CONFESSIONS OF A SURGEON

To Trudie
who made everything possible

George B Mair

Confessions of a Surgeon

Futura Publications Limited

A Futura Book

First published in Great Britain in 1974
by William Luscombe Publisher Limited
First Futura Publications edition 1975
Copyright © George B Mair 1974

ISBN 0 8600 72215
Printed in Great Britain by
Hazell Watson & Viney Ltd
Aylesbury, Bucks

Futura Publications Limited
49 Poland Street
London W1A 2LG

CONTENTS

ACKNOWLEDGEMENT

Thanks are given to Doctor Alistair Mair for permission to use one of his unpublished poems and extracts from his letters.

The author also wishes to express his gratitude to Ann Gore, Strawberry House, Barnes for invaluable assistance in launching this book and to Norrie Smyth of *Glasgow Evening Citizen* for constructive advice bearing upon the manuscript.

He also owes a special debt to Mr William Luscombe for unfailing courtesy and invaluable help in publishing these confessions.

INTRODUCTION

Autobiographies are an impertinence unless they have something to say which is of genuine interest to a mass of people, while confessions are inexcusable unless they expose secrets which bear upon 'public interest'. Also, they are not without danger to the author, because autobiographies are frequently the hall-mark of vanity and confessions usually pin-point an exhibitionist.

Even so, this book is a compressed autobiography laced with confessions and justified only because the whole blend of events deals with secrets which matter.

A number of colleagues will be irritated, but their reaction should measure success or failure in describing attitudes which have usually been ignored. Chiefly, I suppose, because doctors still rate as sacred cows, even if not quite so sacred as forty years ago. The book should also prove how, dating from the early fifties, the public has, really and truly, 'never had it so good', and that in spite of fashionable nostalgia for the 'good old days'.

Legends have grown around the old-style family doctor, but many were really honours graduate con-men with an approach to patients basically similar to that of any well organised New Guinean witch-doctor. Suggestion, faith (of the patient) and physical examinations which were little more than the laying on of hands, were standard. It is also fact that many pink bottles or white powders fulfilled the same purpose as alligator saliva or powdered snake brain, both being used only to buy time while Mother Nature did her healing work in her own orderly style.

The truth is that, with the exception of surgeons, doctors were seldom able to 'cure' anything until the first antibiotic was developed, since when abuse from all sides has created sinister problems. These confessions help to explain how all this came about and how it might have been avoided. They will also suggest why modern surgeons are technically less impressive than in 'the old days', yet why, in spite of this contradiction, surgery is now less dangerous than ever before and why a small talent may take even a little man quite a long way.

As for sex! The inability of most doctors to cope with ignorance, fears or frustrations because of their own built-in prejudices and fundamental lack of knowledge has, for very long, been a tragedy. The sex scene has, therefore, been discussed from several levels, even though conclusions will not only offend some people but irritate many more when they discover that most nurses and practitioners have avoided facing up to their responsibilities simply because they do not know the answers and did not want even to be involved.

Other peculiar professional or governmental attitudes are also outlined and predictable critics will abrade me 'more in sorrow than in anger' while they damn me as a cynic. It may bring the confessions more into focus if I deny cynicism and claim to be one of Fortune's favourites, though personal revelations proving this are intended to show only how the experiences affected my approach to patients. The confessions do, however, lift just one small corner of a curtain to hint at a treasured love story and the sort of secure home life without which no soul can get off the ground.

I have also been preoccupied with a personal need to find Wisdom and have used this small history to explain at least a few milestones which did bring me more close to an elusive target.

Medicine has taught me why Giles draws cartoons as he does, why Aristophanes was a bestseller, why Breughel painted as he did and why the Christian bible is wrong in not emphasising that God simply must have a sense of humour.

It also taught me to respect the courage of uncomplicated people who continue, somehow, to struggle on, and even to walk quite tall during a period when so many others seem to have gone schizoparanoic mad.

One group of people who do not 'struggle on' for too long are, in sad fact, doctors. Average professional life span is only twenty years for men, and most die from a stress disease. In other words, their patients kill them, which, on balance, may be quite reasonable since, throughout the centuries, many patients have been killed by their doctors. It is this last fact which chiefly prompted me to write these 'confessions'.

1 CONFLICT

I removed my first stomach at Fulham Hospital, London, in 1940 while a junior nurse held Rodney Maingot's textbook of *Abdominal Operations* open by my side.

I had never seen a partial gastrectomy performed, so a guide-book was essential. I had, however, collected a number of parchment 'qualifications', and was a Bachelor of Medicine and Bachelor of Surgery (Glasgow 1936), a Doctor of Medicine (Glasgow 1939), and a fellow of the Royal College of Surgeons (Edinburgh 1939). I had also been appointed Resident Surgical Officer, and although greener than the green, green, grass of home, it was acceptable to all concerned that I be let loose upon an unsuspecting chronic duodenal ulcer with serious complications. The patient, of course, took it for granted that I could cope. After all, my white coat and hospital status, plus the fact that nurses (or even sisters) called me 'Sir', saw to that! The operation lasted for just over three hours, but the anaesthetist, who had seen almost every form of butchery, was reassuring – and his judgement was proven sound when the patient recovered. Success momentarily went to my head as I felt that I had 'arrived'.

More important, I knew that my parents would also realise that I had 'arrived', and since they knew nothing of Medicine, except that it was a 'noble profession', they would be delighted, which was a good thing, since the whole idea had been theirs in the first place.

At seventeen I had wished to be a parson, but my father was haunted by memory of childhood poverty endured within a but and ben at Cross Hands, three miles out of Mauchline, Ayrshire, so the church was not even considered. But he shared every (then) successful business man's contempt for 'trade' and believed that a medical degree was passport to social respect and financial security. Which was understandable, since, during the thirties, middle-class Scotland was still convinced that any university qualification was a gateway to all things bright and beautiful in this world, and church membership (with payment of pew rent) insurance against complications in the next. It made sense, from my parents' angle, to prod their sons into medicine, even if the thought of doctors made me wish physically to vomit.

A very senior anaesthetist who knew my father well said recently that 'he was a man who dispensed fragrance wherever he went'. I did not, myself, quite see him in that light. He did, however, dispense tough punishment, using a leather belt which hung behind a pantry door at home, and my mother also wielded telling blows, even if her aim was less sure and her tawse often welted me across the face instead of neck or knees.

Mother was a tough late Victorian with rich auburn hair even when she died in her early eighties, and her face could occasionally look like that of a madonna in spite of her devotion to corporal punishment. She was fascinated by doctors, and her hero was a military-looking person who flaunted a black frock coat around Troon, then a haven of millionaires, where I was born on May 27th, 1914. Doctor Roxburgh condescended towards children and scared me enough to cause nightmares which followed a consistent pattern in that he either chased me with gleaming instruments or else tried to run me down with his motor-car – and in those days motor-cars were almost as rare as the dodo.

Mother, like all adult females within my circle, also regarded sex as the devil does Holy Water, a fact which I did not realise until disaster first struck at Mauchline's infant school when a teacher mentioned Cleopatra's bath in asses' milk. The story appealed to me, but the family went berserk when they heard of the 'obscenity'.

Asses, I was told, did not produce milk. Alternatively, if they did, it was wrong to talk about it.

Their series of state visits to school ended only when an exasperated teacher thrashed me on some other pretext and I began to develop strong views about the morality of striking a person unable to retaliate. But the ass milk episode was a mere bagatelle, the heavens really trembled following a Christmas party during which I paid forfeit after losing a spin-the-plate episode. The forfeit was an 'aeroplane kiss', and it was shared with a comely six-year-old called Lily McCulloch. Technique was simple, a child could do it . . . and did! The parties concerned each hold one end of a piece of string in the mouth. By sucking or drawing it into the mouths heads draw closer, lips meet, and presto! – the aeroplane kiss.

I was indicted on two counts. Why had I kissed a girl at all? But, granted that I did have to pay forfeit, why had I not chosen an ugly girl?

The suggestion may sound absurd, but I probably became a doctor because that aeroplane kiss taught me so clearly how the only way to peace lay in toeing parental line without question. This message had been driven home, and it stayed home.

Other incidents conditioned me even more to think twice before speaking, as for example when I was between seven and eight and mother was bathing me. 'What is that, Mummie?' I said, pointing to my tiny penis, an organ about which I had begun to speculate. A stinging slap proved that this subject was also forbidden and a further interview with my father underlined the point, especially when he called me a 'dirty little bugger'.

My father seldom swore, and I recall him using that word only twice – the other occasion being ten years later when I had delayed his entry into the bathroom. When I finally drew the bolt he was white with anger and used the same phrase, although I had no idea what was bugging him until a boy at school gave me a garbled tutorial on masturbation, adding that my 'old man must be right one he must'.

Life was confused. Questions about anything really perplexing were tabu, but new tabus appeared with every passing month and Nemesis struck if I did not spot them in time.

Oddly enough, at about this stage, the mystery of death began to intrigue me and may even have made the idea of a medical future less objectionable. It began when William Robertson, father of my mother, died during our Mauchline years and his widow, Grandmama (who could never have been called 'granny') claimed that on the night after he died he returned to her saying, 'Mary, when your time comes I'll let you know in advance and meet you.' Seven surviving daughters and one son, Alex, accepted this story, as they accepted everything

3

their mother ever said, and felt temporarily reassured about life on the Other Side.

As a matter of interest, and to round off the incident, years later when I was a medical student an apparently normal Grandmama did summon the family to an earlier-than-usual Christmas party and did announce that 'Willie' had promised to come for her that very evening. She then said farewell to each of her grandchildren separately and died on schedule, with a style which struck me as being very civilised and most creditable.

Meanwhile, at Troon, Alex' wife, Elice, then a very young bride, took me into the bedroom where Grandpa lay in his coffin and said 'doesn't he look nice?'

He did. Nicer, in fact, than the dandy-martinet I remembered who kept scores of canaries and ran a licensed grocery in Glasgow, but whose word, I discovered many years later, had always been his bond. A number of aunts then arrived with mother, and Elice horrified them by saying 'you must kiss Papa goodbye'. She leaned forward as she spoke and kissed him gently on the forehead while the others stood by and said in chorus 'You can't do that, it isn't nice for the boy.'

I was amazed. Elice was, and still is a gracious person, her lips were warm and soft, and since it seemed reasonable to kiss the old man goodbye I wondered what happened after death that his daughters could refuse to kiss him. So death began to intrigue me.

I had already discovered that it could strike fast when my father had taken me with him on a business trip to Belfast in 1920 during 'the troubles'. We were near the station in a tram when it jerked to a halt. People dropped to the floor as shots snapped out. Since we had no experience of this sort of situation my father and I were the last to move, and we both saw a pedestrian fall to the sidewalk with blood spurting around his face. Later, when the shooting had subsided, I overheard people say that he had been killed.

I was also familiar with shotguns and remembered especially a weasel which died with macabre ceremony. The beast had crossed our paths near Lawersbridge Farm, Mauchline and a shot only shattered its hind quarters. I can still see it wriggle towards a rock and turn to face its enemies. The little teeth

4

looked like tiny pearls, but the eyes were bloodshot and sparkling with defiance as the men watched it curiously. One of them explained how courageous a weasel could be when cornered. He then lifted a heavy stone, raised it high above the poor creature's head and let it fall. The little animal swayed sideways, but was trapped across its broken hind legs and was finally killed by a second stone dropped from a height of four or five feet. Sometimes, when I am alone, I again hear its dying scream. Maybe this atrocity, more than anything else, provoked the contempt which I still have for people who take life needlessly or cruelly, but I was also forced to wonder what exactly happened when man or beast died and what, if anything, left its body?

By seventeen it was taken for granted that I would do as I was told and become a doctor. I gathered that this would enable me to run a big car, be important in any community and earn good money – three tribal totems which I knew mattered greatly.

Before enrolling for classes in Glasgow my father's mother, Granny (who could never have been called 'grandmama') died in 1931, and my father decided to visit his brother Willie in Boston, U.S.A. I was detailed to accompany him and we sailed from Glasgow on board the *Cameronia*.

Our journey produced a few peak moments – starting after disembarkation when my father refused to join a queue under a notice marked ALIENS. His exchanges with an Irish-American policeman swiftly taught us both that American police are different from the British.

Our composure was also shattered in New York when two men carrying violin cases entered a lounge of the MacAlpine Hotel and shortly afterwards mowed down a new arrival wearing slouch hat and blue suit with padded shoulders. Their exit was unhurried and no one raised an eyebrow since gangster killings were then *à la mode*.

We became unpopular with staff because my father refused to place an order for 'hooch' with the senior bell-hop. This was also normal routine in the 'prohibition' era, and anyone who did not conform was considered more anti-social than gangsters who knocked off a citizen in the public area of a respectable hotel.

We were innocents abroad, though my father found it hard to

5

convince a security officer of our innocence when we entered a 'wrong' bedroom in Buffalo. A young woman was sitting, more or less naked, on the bed, and her screams might have been heard from coast to coast. However, she made no effort to cover herself, and I was able, for the first time, to confirm at leisure that female breasts have a magical appeal. It was also the first time I had seen anyone with a good all-over tan. Just as I was beginning to regret our British climate a security officer arrived with a rush, gun in hand, and shouting a sentence beginning 'say, you!' When we finally left the room explanations were being given to the girl, still unclad. 'Screwy, babe! We get them all sorts here. But move over, will yah.'

Travel, I felt, was a good idea!

At Niagara I met a man who made a good living by selling photographs of himself at various stages – being nailed inside a barrel, to poising on the brink of the Falls, bobbing in the spray half way down, being picked up by *Maid of the Mist,* and finally being garlanded with flowers by beautiful girls. This incident sowed seeds of an idea that bread could be earned through ways more interesting than medicine and I filed the fact for possible future use.

Distinguished-looking Indians in full war paint on one reservation also made me decide to study exotica as a hobby and to make 'travel' a second string to my professional bow, while glimpses of off-beat bars around Times Square clinched a decision which was eventually carried out in detail.

Matters really blew up, however, during our return voyage on *Letitia* after a kindly parson had enquired about my academic qualifications. Since they were of minimal standard I threw in a few extra credits, never suspecting that he would congratulate my father on his brilliant son. I was all but disowned, made to apologise to the flustered parson and kept more or less out of circulation for the duration of the voyage.

Back home in 'Cessnock', Kilmarnock, I could think only of Granny. I missed her . . . and I still miss her. She was five feet two, of wiry peasant stock and afraid of neither life nor death. When a friend was about to emigrate to Australia in the 1890s Granny walked miles in order to give the girl her own life savings to help pay the passage, and ten shillings plus nine pence meant a deal of money in those days, especially to a young mother with seven children to feed and a signalman husband who earned only around thirty shillings per week. Granny also knew her Classics, as well as her Burns and Scott. She could recite *Marmion* by the yard and her eyes lit up with fire when she came to the lines:

> 'Charge, Chester! Charge!
> On Stanley on,'
> Were the last words
> of Marmion.

When her local minister, the Reverend Wilson Baird, first came to Mauchline United Presbyterian Church his oldest elder, as a child, had seen Robert Burns (or so it was said!). The Reverend had 'almost' first-hand stories of Burns, and Granny knew them all. Mossgiel Farm of mouse fame was only an hour's walk away and Poosie Nancy's Howff was one of the local pubs. She even claimed that various old folk in the parish had mothers sired by Burns when coming through the rye. [The 'original' version did not say 'kiss a body, comin' thro' the rye'. The verb was much more specific.]

Granny lived long enough to see the Burns cult get into overdrive, but looked on with contempt. 'Robbie wouldn't hae sat down wi' any of them,' she used to say. 'They just use his memory as an excuse to get drunk.' Twenty years later my father was saying even more of the same thing, and, on balance I agree, but as a doctor I discovered the human need to contrive 'peak moments', and at least the Burns cult gives Scots open licence to let off steam.

Granny also respected George Douglas Brown, that strange man from Ochiltree, Ayrshire, who wrote the *House with the Green Shutters*. Indeed, when she first saw me squawking on my mother's knees she named me on the spot. 'There lies wee George Douglas Brown Mair.' The Douglas part was removed after days of negotiation, but I was never allowed to forget the tie-up, and ten Mauchline years were lived out in the shadows of mighty literary figures.

I was her last visitor. She died suddenly and I wept in secret when I heard the news. Her death made me even more interested to learn more about a great mystery. Everyone I knew was scared sick of death and only Grandmama, Granny and the weasel had gone out with the flag flying. The weasel had been defiant to the end while Granny had never even mentioned death except to say on one winter's evening when we were discussing Burns: 'I'm looking forward to a word with Rabbie afterwards. I'd like to know why he was so damnt happy about dining wi' a lord.'

Death, for her, was a simple affair. Everyone did it. She had taken four or five hours off work to produce her first baby – and she seems to have taken only a few seconds to die. She was a great lady who loved children and despised phonies. At seventeen I also remembered that she had not been enthusiastic about doctors either.

An old-style family doctor served Mauchline until the early '20s. He wore a grey-black frock coat, homespun greyish pants and a greeny-black bowler hat. Children and dogs loved Doctor Reid, but he steadily lost 'paying' patients to Doctor Allan of Catrine, a small hunchback with a face upon which you could break rocks and who scared me even more than mother's hero in Troon. He charged more than Doctor Reid and he lived further away, which, by and large, is the criterion still influencing tribes in Melanesia or Africa, where the best witch-doctor is the one who charges most pigs (or cows) and who lives in another village.

Scarlet fever is now comparatively unimportant, but during the twenties in Mauchline it was a potential killer. Victims were carted off to Kilmarnock Infectious Diseases Hospital in a black cab driven by a squat little man with a purple face and bulbous nose. The horses were black and the whole set-up would have appealed to Hitchcock. No more sinister-looking buggy ever jolted through the streets of Mauchline, and it terrified me.

The hunchback in Catrine also held strong views about rearing children and I once overheard him advise my mother to 'stand no nonsense. Leather him if he doesn't show respect'. He probably did not know that Grandmama gave much the same advice to any daughter with a new infant. 'Rule that child,' she would say, 'or the child will rule you.' Not that there were too many babies around! The seven daughters produced only six children and Elice had but one owing to health problems after the birth which made her husband react by adding cat's whiskers and ears to his bride on their wedding photographs. A petulant, bilious act reflecting the man within.

Curiosity about where children came from had also made medicine more attractive as a possible career even when I was very young, because although the family stuck to official party policy in saying that 'they had been found underneath the rhubarb', I never really believed them.

Oddly enough, the absurdity of this simile never touched me until years later, when I heard one uncle refer to a dog's penis as 'its bit of rhubarb', in which case there was a valid comparison, because the babies would also have been sired *underneath* the rhubarb since it is a million dollars to a brass button that variations in posture would not have been tolerated and that when 'doing their duty' each daughter probably closed her eyes and thought of the Empire while in the classical position with the male dominant. It is a sound bet that most of these daughters reversed the ideal recipe for happy marriage and were aristocrats in the kitchen, devils in the drawing-room (when in private) and economists in bed.

Sex was always the ultimate sin and after Granny's death a test experiment proved the point when I set a trap by writing girls' names in a small diary, added what might have been addresses in code and rounded off, on days when I knew that my parents had been out for an evening, by jotting down figures like 6.30 or 8.15.

The experiment was successful. When I left the diary inside my desk I returned one evening to face the high court in full session. It became clear that my belongings had been searched and that the campaign was still on to protect me from the demon sex.

Who were these girls?

Had I ever kissed them?

Correction from my mother. 'Had I ever touched them?'

Had I been familiar? This from my father.

A side remark to God also asked what they had done to deserve this, and my silence was interpreted as insolence. The whole episode was humiliating but revenge was sweet.

Later that evening I opened one from a set of ten volumes of Arthur Mee's *Children's Encyclopaedia*. They had been a gift from my parents, though I am certain they would never have been bought had they realised how beautifully certain volumes would be illustrated with photographs of Greek sculpture. I concentrated upon nude female goddesses and for the first time in their lives my parents were confronted with a situation about which they could do nothing since the Greeks were respectable, or clearly they would not have been in the book.

Years passed before I began to appreciate how the chilly ice of bigoted puritanism had removed all thoughts of pleasure from sex, or how frustrated adults equated sex with sin. This childhood experience made me more than usually willing, as a doctor, to involve myself with such people and attempt to straighten out at least some of their problems. Now, thinking back over it, I would rate that aspect of my medical work as easily the most emotionally rewarding. It is difficult for younger people during these later 20th century years to appreciate how little their own parents knew of sex when their age, or to understand the fears most older people experienced until comparatively recently. [Very many, it seems, still do.]

Virginity was a possession to be prized above all things. I still remember the aeroplane kiss. 'Why didn't you choose an ugly girl?' I know that a bow-legged, toothless, adenoidal virgin would then rate in the minds of most women as an infinitely more suitable bride for any son than an experienced, bedworthy, busty and warm-hearted wench with plenty of everything in the right places.

To be a bastard was probably worse than to be a wife-beating jail-bird or advanced alcoholic, yet I also realised, even at seventeen, how cruel it was to make such a judgement. Where was the compassion one heard so much about in church?

I was unconsciously becoming anti-church, anti-any-establishment, anti-violence and anti-any-profession.

During the twenties there was a hang-over of feudalism in Britain and the local Big House meant something. An invitation to tea by the laird's wife was the ultimate accolade for women like my mother, and during one such occasion I let her down badly. I was only seven when the great lady herself asked, in Ballochmyle House, 'how about the wee laddie giving a recitation, Mrs Mair?'

This was standard routine and mother expected me to stand up in the centre of the room with hands by my side and recite:

'*A Child's Evening Prayer*'
by Samuel Taylor Coleridge.

'E're on my bed my limbs I lay,
God grant me grace my prayers to say:
Oh God! Preserve my mother dear
In strength and health for many a year.

And, O! Preserve my father too,
And may I pay him reverence due;
And may I my best thoughts employ
To be my parents' hope and joy.'

I felt that the lines lacked punch, and unexpectedly remembered a story which had come my way at school. I even managed to explain the change of programme and went on to my big scene at a time when, it must be remembered, motor-cars were extremely uncommon, and any story involving a car had, automatically, to be exciting.

'A man left a motor-car in charge of a Chinaman while he went into a pub for a drink. The car was on a little hill, but when he came out the motor had disappeared. The man asked the Chinese boy where it had gone and he replied:

'Me no know.
Me no idea.
Me press a button
And it go like diarrhoea!'

The lady of the Big House was dressed in a purple velvet gown and white shawl. A large cameo brooch sat across her bosom and a string of pearls lay round her neck. They all quivered as she heaved with emotion until, finally, she laughed . . . and laughed . . . until the tears ran down her cheeks. My mother then took the hint and also laughed, if only for a few moments. Later, after the evening meal, I was 'dealt with' and sent to bed, but it shook me a little to find how bitter I still was even after ten years had passed and I vowed that diarrhoea

11

would crop up fairly often in conversation before I had long been at medical school. I must have been very childish!

Purchase of my first long trousers was celebrated by taking a sentimental walk round Kilmarnock where we had lived since I was ten. It would, I felt sure, be a nostalgic saunter with memories of happy days.

In fact it began and ended at Kilmarnock Academy, where, for the life of me, I could remember only sadistic teachers and sorrow. The belt had been used, not for misdemeanours, but for failure to understand. It was the first resort of inadequate personalities. A person called Law, nicknamed Jinkie, was one of the worst offenders, and I still see him leaning against a classroom wall with his left arm while he beat boy after boy with his right. Not for insolence, not for bad manners, not for swearing, but simply because of errors in syntax or construction. Oddly enough, none of us had feared him, we had only despised him.

The School area dissolved into a mixed up mess of memory – stinking lavatories, bullies who threw people into the 'freezer' at the swimming pool, pupils tormenting Catholic children on their way to their own school across the road, and many men who were mediocrities but who ruled classes through fear rather than respect.

Sandy Clark, who coped with Latin, was one of the few exceptions, and his friendship, now forty years old, is probably the only good thing which came to me from the Academy. The blur of school memories was replaced by a strange moment of dramatic revelation when I seemed to see all seventeen years as an infinite number of still pictures flitting across my eyes until I finally did accept that I had seldom been happy.

Some of the following pictures were to influence my professional and private attitudes profoundly.

Hunger marchers passing through Mauchline on their way to London while upper crust village ladies organised soup kitchens! I know now that some of these men were dying on their feet. It is, even today, impossible to forget their famine-ravaged faces, but how many professional trouble-makers now realise how far Labour has travelled in one generation? How many even want to know?

12

Cows dead from foot and mouth disease! The smoke of burning meat floated across the village and still tingles my nostrils.

Lord Overton of Overton Farm riding home drunk on a Saturday night! He is so vivid that many of Hogarth's etchings repel even today, and I see his face as only Hogarth could draw it. He was a revolting Dickensian character who did more than anyone to keep me from ever running any risk of being hooked on alcohol.

And there was the farmer who bought the funeral feast for his wife before she had died. When he returned to the farm from Kilmarnock market he flung open the bedroom door. Mother and I were sitting beside the dying woman as he stood with a ham under one arm and a bottle sticking out from a pocket. His boots were dirty brown after walking through the byre, and he could not believe his eyes. 'Ye stupid bitch,' he shouted. 'Why the Hell are ye no' dead yet?'

There was also a farm kitchen and a man spouting blood from his wrist! A hand had been severed by a threshing machine and the stump looked hideous. While we were waiting for Doctor Alexander of Galston a son arrived holding something. 'Here's your hand, faither,' he said. The farmer glanced up. 'Gie it tae the dog,' and laughed when an old collie sniffed for a second at the bloody end before looking reproachfully towards its master.

I also saw an amiable taxi-driver, who used to let me sit on his knee and steer his cab, after he had destroyed himself using a humane-killer from the slaughterhouse. I wondered why. This, like almost all my memory pictures, was as sad-making and grim as that of Harvey the solicitor, who had shot himself twice!

Death it seemed, had plagued me in Mauchline and I pictured again every house with drawn blinds when a hearse passed. Death was something upon which everyone drew blinds and I wondered if doctors knew anything more about it than anyone else. Forty years later I am still wondering.

My brother Alistair, now an author and playwright, is ten years and two weeks younger than myself. My moments of revelation outside the school also told me that his arrival had probably been unwanted. An early bronchopneumonia had been followed by 'asthma', and Cessnock stank of Friar's balsam, mustard poultices and eucalyptus oil. We had lived in Mauchline until his arrival in 1924, and earlier memories suddenly became even more vivid.

Drunks on the main streets on any afternoon or evening.

Hungry men waiting at The Cross for the dole.

The day when a well-dressed man stopped me and asked: 'where the hell can I get a pee?' And cuffed me when I didn't understand.

Men from Ballochmyle quarries returning home with grey faces encrusted with red sandstone dust: and coughing their guts out.

Dry privies stinking beneath clouds of bluebottle flies.

A hearse which went to the cemetery with one corpse and returned with four paralytic drunks inside.

Men in pubs shouting damnation to the new flying machines.

And, for a second, my still flashes even had a sound track as I heard raw bellowing voices roar out Scotland's pathetic toast which may have encouraged more vandalism than people realise.

> 'Here's tae us!
> Wha's like us?
> Damn't few!
> And they're a' deid.'

There was fear everywhere. Fear of the poor-house. Fear of gossip. Fear of poverty. Fear of the devil. Fear of Catholics. Fear of Death. Even fear of poor old Doctor Reid, who lost so many of his 'paying' patients to the hunchback.

But the second greatest fear was fear of the poor-house.

I also heard again the nervous laughter of women listening to faint noises from the village's first radio. 'Devil's kisses,' said one woman wrapped in a grey shawl as a 'cat's whisker' made the machine crackle and crickle like witch's laughter.

But the *Four Horsemen of the Apocalypse* brought real terror, and a pale cinema manager stopped the show to explain that noises of battle were only 'sound effects' made by local people to 'make the picture seem more real'. This is my first memory of mass hysteria, and I did not care for it, though I disliked even more the night when scores of villagers walked to 'the top of the

Hill' to wait for the End of the World while others jeered, spat or cursed.

I, personally, at the age of seven or eight had been 'saved' by Evangeline Booth during an evangelical campaign in Ayrshire with her trendy-looking son, who played swinging accordion music, and I wondered, next day, why I felt no different. Perhaps I did not 'believe' enough. The theme song was

> 'Only believe.
> Only believe.
> All things are possible.
> Only believe.'

I never heard it sung properly until thirty years later, on Saint Lucia, when a Caribbean steel band, at my request, gave it the full treatment on a shimmering beach underneath a full moon. I found it difficult, in Mauchline, to believe in anything. On the Caribbean islands it is difficult not to believe in everything, especially when the locals laugh and 'make a joyful noise'. But that lay decades ahead, as part of a future which the puzzled seventeen-year-old on that day could not even begin to visualise when fifteen years of memory were compressed into as many seconds of vivid, wide-angle, high-speed colour stills.

Clydesdale horses in full fig drawing hay-carts loaded with children off to a picnic made the only note of light relief. That, and my visit from a fairy. I believed, and still do, that I saw a fairy, that I touched her and that the experience to some extent changed my life. She was a most fetching little creature with quivering, yellowish wings, long pale hair and sleek, trailing legs. She danced around my face and shoulders for several minutes while I was sitting alone in woods near Cessnock burn. She was the most beautiful thing I have ever seen and I felt good just to be near her. When she touched me or darted near my hands or cheeks I felt a deeply satisfying sense of peace. When she finally flitted into the bushes I almost wept. Something, way above the normal run of things, had happened to me and I felt really privileged. I still refuse to believe that 'she was only a butterfly'.

This experience made me realise that the impossible can, and

15

does, happen, and when a person is able to accept such a situation then he has crashed an important barrier.

My fairy proved the reality of life in other dimensions.

Depressed by most of the memory pictures conjured up in Kilmarnock I modified my 'end-of-school-chapter' plans and cycled down to Troon to see where I had been born and where Grandpa died, but when I stood on the front, outside Fir Brae House, I could recall only a thrashing from the old man for having left a dining-room because I yukked at the sight of tripe and onions and quit without saying 'please may I leave the table?'

Then I recalled his canaries, scores of them in tiny cages singing their hearts out while the old *bon viveur* watched and listened with satisfaction. 'Why don't you let them out, Grandpapa? It can't be nice in a cage.' A smile, and a pat on the head. 'We're all in cages, boy, and don't you forget it. But canaries sing, and so can I – still! Make sure you do the same.'

I didn't know what he meant at the time, but the story became important when I did.

Fir Brae was the gathering place of our 'clan', which is to say, the Robertsons. My favourite aunt was Mary, a small, dumpy woman with a heart of pure gold. Her husband, Bob Young, apologised one day for a late arrival. 'We missed the train, Mama. I got into a fankle lacing up Mary's stays.' He said this so naturally that I now realise he might, just might, be an exception, and have been fairly happily married. But the aunts shushed him to silence. 'Don't say things like that in front of the children.'

At seventeen I knew that I had everything to learn and accepted that there was an adult conspiracy to suppress knowledge. At seventeen I also suspected that most of the world wore a mask. Within a few years of becoming a doctor I knew it to be true, though the shock of discovering what lay behind the mask was sick-making. Yet I would never have believed, when preparing for the university, that no one there or in hospital would ever be able to prepare me for what lay behind the average mask. There seems to be a tacit understanding among academics that it is better to throw students in at the deep end. It is also a fact that too many recent academics have never,

16

themselves, been thrown in even at the shallow end, but have passed most of their professional lives over-protected and insulated against the world. Many who have come my way in recent years know little more (outside their subject) than I knew at, say twenty-three, and I believe that they opted for an academic routine because they hadn't the guts to face up to the realities of broad-spectrum living. How can teachers of that ilk create 'whole' men?

The Right Reverend Doctor Leonard Small was our family minister in Kilmarnock and now glows with distinction in Edinburgh. Few could have presented the Christian message with greater sincerity or skill, yet I went to college believing that official Christian dogma was an angled corruption of truth.

On the political front I also believed, even at seventeen, that politicians on every level were, in modern jargon, either, frontmen, fall-guys, chisellers, con-men or a combination of all four, and that only a minority were likely to be sincere. On a different level, my father repeatedly said that he had yet to meet either an educated or intelligent local authority councillor, and I almost agree. A few are triers and start with ideals, but they are mostly doomed, eventually, by British preference for mediocrity.

I returned home from my Troon pilgrimage sensing that I had begun to get a few ideas straight. I was suspicious of aggressive adults and detested brutality. I distrusted most small-town behaviour patterns, and doubted the sincerity of almost everyone when self-interest became involved. I suspected the sincerity of any authority, doubted the ability of the Church to remove fear of either life or death, believed that sex must be a 'good thing' since most adults condemned it, and appreciated that most people were both lonely and afraid. I was also vaguely worried about the past. Instinct told me that my memory pictures should have shown more than people oppressed by fear and that there had been too much thought of death.

However, I did believe in fairies and this was an enormous leap forward, since it also meant that I accepted the reality of life 'elsewhere'. I vowed that in the years ahead I would live to the full, create my own sunshine, and forget about death until a time came when I would have to meet it on its own terms, and that when the time came my memory pictures would then be bright enough to help me through to the next level of development. I even began to thrill at the thought of a long future among people who would know how to laugh.

2 PARENTS WHO WERE 'ALMOST' . . .

Medicine, I found, involved more than pill-pushing or reaching for a knife, the human angle was more important, and my father taught me more than any lecturer at medical school. He was a small dark man with a blackish-brown moustache and was as tough as whip-cord. He showed no sentiment within the family and told only one story about a moment of personal indiscretion.

He had escorted a girl home after a dance, way back about 1905, and believed that she was expecting him to kiss her goodnight. She lived on an upper flat reached by an outside stair, but when he dived for her cheek he slipped and fell, finishing in mud at the bottom of the steps while the girl laughed 'fit to crack a rib' right at the top. He picked himself up and limped five miles home. The story may explain much of his undoubted fear for women.

When he died during his eighty-first year a number of unexpected items were found on his book-shelves. One was a volume entitled *What every young man should know about Women*. The other was *What a man should know about women of forty*. Thank Fortune, nowadays, for *Nova*, for *She*, for *Forum*, *Playboy*, *Penthouse* and many others.

These stupid late Victorian books and his sad, abortive kiss, probably explained in part his attitudes to sex. Indirectly, they may also have influenced my own attitudes until I had learned at least a little sense.

A few of his oft-repeated sayings eventually became invaluable:

'It's not the beginning of life which counts. It's the end.'

'No man can be happy unless he is able to look anyone in the eye and tell them to go to hell without worrying about consequences.'

'The surest way to make an enemy is to put someone under an obligation.'

'Anyone who expects either gratitude or thanks in this world is potty.'

'No man is ever dispassionately generous. He gives only because it makes him feel better.'

'A husband should make sure that his wife is never short of money even if he has to go short himself.'

'A man knows only what he has read, what he has seen, what he has been told and what he has experienced. Most of us are too scared to experience much, which makes it difficult to believe anything.'

He died smoking a cigar, alone, as he would have wanted it. He never wished to cause trouble, and he valued privacy on important occasions. He was a great man. He was almost a *really* great man.

Mother's world was her kitchen, her sisters, a few friends, the church guilds and her grandchildren.

She was almost beautiful and probably would have been really beautiful had she been born within a different sort of society or time period where natural things came and were done naturally. Her sex hang-ups were not unique, but they were sad and tainted several lives, while her possessiveness for my brother Alistair after he developed asthma was tragic. If a senior doctor had not interfered and caused him to go to boarding-school, he might, he recently said, have matured into a masochistic homosexual.

I owe her much – and my patients probably owed her more.

She virtually drove me (in all innocence) towards study of sex on a global basis, and I know now that if I had a son of eighteen or nineteen needing help in a foreign country I would advise him to state the case to any youngish prostitute (British excepted), rather than to any embassy, consulate, amateur do-gooder or 'sensible' family friend. Whores, as the Church calls them, know the ropes and are *sympatique*. They would be more likely to help out with no strings attached. My increasing knowledge of puritanical perversities, tribal obsessions with flagellation and bigoted ignorance of the sex drive was eventually appreciated by scores of teenagers, exasperated, as I had been, by unreasonable puritanical hang-ups within their own society.

Yet mother had one attribute beyond price. Her instinct was

very fine, and it was enough for me if she listened to a problem and said simply: 'something tells me you should (or shouldn't) do so-and-so'. This also gave me an awareness of forces which had a bearing on later medical life, and I learned, eventually, to love her as I learned in time to love my father. Perhaps her one great contribution to my development was, all unconscious, to teach me the importance of instinct – of 'hunches'.

Now, with a little maturity and when I know more about how people tick, I miss them both. Fear was their kill-joy. Something terrible was always due to happen tomorrow, if not sooner. Their personal problems must have been fiery acid and I now pity them in many ways. But I also love them. They were people with standards, standards about which they were sincere, and they were, far beyond the average, selfless. 'Others' always came first in their thoughts. But one of their personal ambitions began to be fulfilled when classes started in October 1931.

It is only remarkable that among the many 'others' who came first in their thoughts they never paused to consider their own unwisdom in forcing their family along paths which were sign-posted SORROW. A recent letter from my brother Alistair in Australia highlights a few of his own still passionate emotions.

23rd October, 1973.

. . . Does it truly matter if surviving family members are dis-pleased (by your book?). Let's *live* the rest of our lives, be honest, or are we for ever to be haunted by the ghosts of yesterday, even if some of them are still alive? I hope Elice will see the book if only because she'll be delighted to see truth at last after almost a lifetime of hypocrisy – not to men-tion cruelty and other facets. . . .

Everything is all now a far cry from 'Cessnock' (our family home in Kilmarnock). And, to interpose, I often ask myself what Cessnock was. To me, I guess it represented a degree of security materially I've never known since. It offered an average standard of living I've never known since. And many other things. But always I find myself saying – yes, sure, but: how quite enervating, personality destroying, utterly, totally and destructively dull. Then when I say that, I find myself ad-ding – wouldn't you rather have that than trauma after trauma, excitement after excitement, insecurity, uncertainty – both emotional and moneywise – and so on, and the answer comes back – astonishingly – No! No, no, no! I'd rather have what I've got and what I've had! Because I've lived. I've at least laid my tongue on the edge of the world and tasted it a bit.

To continue. I think with compassion of our parents, married in, I think, 1911. Mum died in 1964. That's one hell of a long time. And what happened in the interval? To Dad – plenty. He made good starting from scratch. To Mum? Nothing. Two children. Commonplace. Utterly commonplace. Which is not meant to sound snob, but simply that it happens to lots of other people. In terms of living and knowing what living is all about, nothing. Not that I know what it is all about. Who does? But how incredibly dull. 54 years of marriage, without, I suspect, the slightest idea of the meaning of the word 'love' beyond 'warm affection'. How did Mum ever get pregnant, I sometimes ask myself? What an incredible way to spend half a century or more. Yet . . . Yet . . . And again – yet. I recall a coal fire, and Dad with his slippers off, and the wireless (*sic*) going for the nine o'clock news, and a maid coming in with supper, and how sensible and reasonable and attractive it all seems in retrospect. In my slushy moments, the thought would make me homesick, or whatever the *mot juste* is for *temps perdus*. Almost all the time I shriek for freedom from just that. Yet – how comforting it is in memory. But it was bloody awful in reality. Where you couldn't bring a girl friend home without her being frozen out. Where you had to report present and correct at 2.00 a.m. after a dance and account for your every movement – an excellent training in being a liar – right up to the age of 27 in my case. Where, when you were aged eight, your mother came in and threw back the sheets and corrected your posture if you were in the normal foetal position, which meant one hand happened to cover your crotch – how utterly obscene and disgusting an attitude. I could go on. I won't, 'cos I know I don't need to. I'll never know how Mum turned out two normal heterosexual males. By rights we should have been either impotent or the biggest fairies in the business. And yet

22

my final reaction is compassion for my mother and considerable affection for my father.

But TROON (the home of my mother's parents and where she grew up under 'Grandmama'). Troon, to me, is the most obscene four (*sic*) letter word in the English language. I'm going to have a ball with grandmama if there is a life after physical death. I regard her, and her influence – continuing – as the most evil I have known in one family. So lose me Troon. I shall never go back, in spite of the fact that our parents' bodies are buried there.

And Dad did NOT die an unwilling agnostic. He died an agnostic. Period. The poor man didn't know why he couldn't 'believe'. He lacked faith and was too rational to know what faith was all about. But he handled the church (small 'c') finances very well. God will no doubt chalk it up on the credit side. Craig's wife, Ann and their daughter Lorna are Catholics. Helen and I are Catholics either manqué or not. Short of North Ireland Protestant homes I can't imagine a more anti-Catholic upbringing than ours. Catholics were filthy slum children who lived in local Council Housing areas. Their status was comparable with the Indian untouchables. I rebelled then. And I rebel now. So maybe our parents have got what they deserved – a fistful of relatives, either by blood, marriage, relationship or belief who are Catholic and proud of it. The Catholic Church has many faults – and I am competent to spell them out – but possibly the biggest fault is to ask too much. And what does the Church of Scotland ask? Damn all, except to stuff 20 cents in the plate, come along to the odd Communion, wear a tie to the Sunday service and you're all right Jack. The Kingdom of Heaven is yours. What a load of rubbish. I have to work. But I have more to say. It may be later today. But right now I've had enough. Forgive me. All love to you all—

Alistair.

My brother's letters can be shattering. Yet he never overstates his case, and, like myself, he wore a mask. It may, perhaps, be to our credit that although sorely provoked on occasion we never revealed our true feelings towards parents who did their best according to their own light. It was our misfortune that the light was often a black darkness born in Troon within a matriarchal home in which Man was a second class citizen. Sometimes, nowadays, I would give most of my possessions to hear their Parish Church minister, long dead of course, deliver a sermon based on the text 'Tell it not in Gath, publish it not in the streets of Askalon'. Did he ever know, I wonder, of the mid-twentieth century Askalon which flourished within his own parish? Male children were to be desired. But were desirable only until puberty. There was a weird but valid basis for comparison between the matriarchal society of Troon's Fir Brae and the 'daughters of the Philistines'. Fir Brae, of course, would not have 'rejoiced' to hear that 'the king is dead'. That particular matriarchal society rested content with demoting him and spiritually emasculating the male offspring so that something inside really did die. And it is that influence which obsesses my brother and causes him to rate it as the most evil he has known in any one family.

The real tragedy, of course, is that everything was done with the best possible intentions – by everyone. There was no conscious evil intent. Only ignorance and deep-down fear of showing physical warmth or passionate affection. It can be understood, I am sure, that I welcomed opportunity to 'escape' and that prospect of university life seemed the only road to some sort of freedom.

3 WHEN STUDENTS WALKED TALL

It was good to be an undergraduate during years before politicians had converted universities into sausage machines for packaging indifferently educated graduates. Glasgow, like others in 1931, provided facilities for training without compulsion to use them, and graduates were quite cultivated people, competent in their own discipline, but also knowing how it related to others, which is more than can be said of most degree men over the last quarter century.

Clearly, to achieve this, their professors had to be men of quality, and the influence of my first Principal, Sir Donald MacAlistair, made itself felt from the beginning when he welcomed students, during a freshmen's dinner, in eighteen languages. He was a gentleman and scholar. Compton Mackenzie was elected Lord Rector and I supported his Nationalist platform chiefly because I had met Ramsay MacDonald in Lossiemouth and not been impressed, but the battle on election day made me conscious, for the first time, of my own strength and virility.

Other battles followed, later in the winter, when a minority of older students made war against Rome. A gang of slum thugs, called the Billy Boys, operated over a city area now rubbed out by the new centrum, and another gang had H.Q. in Partick. Thirty or forty students would occasionally invade the gangs' territories, chanting a slogan which never failed to work. 'Fuck the Pope', was their simple war-cry, and it reflected that crassly stupid built-in religious bigotry which has killed so much joy and so many people over the centuries.

In 1972 Maurice Lindsay referred to the unfortunate results of union between dunted, stunted (and possibly also runted) low I.Q. Irish with Scots on the same level. No one who knows Glasgow or similar areas would argue this, but these students were simply unthinking idiots – a mindless, mini-mob, obsessed by confused religious attitudes instilled by their own families.

25

Extra-curricular activities at least helped to relieve the monotony of first-term subjects which seemed to have no bearing upon 'medicine'. Physics, chemistry, botany and zoology failed to enchant, but we suffered, knowing that better things, anatomy, for instance, lay ahead.

Professor Bryce (Tommy to everyone) had carved a special place in the hall of anatomical fame, when, in 1908, working with Professor Teacher, he isolated a fertilised human ovum only thirteen or fourteen days old. This had been a world-shaking discovery. It still rated so in early 1932 when even very few advanced thinkers had got round to speculating about test-tube babies. We attended his first lecture prepared to sit at the feet of the Master and left knowing that the Master was also 'one of the boys'. His jovial, ruddy face and gleaming eyes twinkled with mischief, and he made the deadest of dead subjects dance into life. We longed to come to grips with the 'origin and insertions' of muscles, 'and fingers itched to grasp scalpel or saw'. A junior demonstrator introduced us to our first anatomical joke. 'What, sir, is the origin and insertion of the longest muscle in the human male subject?'

Silence.

'The penis, twit. It rises along the length of Sauchiehall Street and is inserted in Kelvingrove Park. Which, incidentally, is a sea of heaving buttocks at night. So keep away unless you want to catch the clap.' Since there was a prostitute every few yards along Bath Street, Blythswood Square, West Campbell Street and many others he had a valid point, but I began to suspect that staff had a brief to keep an eye over general morality and hoped they did not overdo things.

Most of us had made an early visit to the laboratories and inspected cadavers laid out like fish on cold, stone slabs. I had even seen the long boxes in which they were stored after arrival. They rested, one on top of the other, stinking of formalin and chemicals, with shaven heads and ivory skin, knobbly knees and eyes like marbles. Collected from the poor-houses, or unclaimed from police morgues of Britain, Ireland and parts of Belgium and France, they had been processed and filed, so that we, and others like us, might one day become medicine men. Sexless, humourless, with less personality than a statue, they had once been the noblest work of God, and Doctor Wyburn, a small dark man with pale face who eventually took over the Chair, was laid on to teach us our obligation to respect the dead.

We rated this lecture as a sop to unknown powers-that-be far in the background, because it was difficult to imagine greater lack of respect than to be laid, naked, on a stone slab, while two students dissected each arm and leg, and another two exposed mysteries of head and neck, and while yet another duet was worked out over a ten week period within thorax and abdomen.

Wyburn gave no specific examples as to how cadavers might be abused, but imagination took over, and in due course throughout five terms I saw young women occasionally skip using a length of small gut, or a couple play baseball with a bone for bat and a kidney for ball. On the first day of one term women made daisy chains and bedecked the subjects as though for carnival, while on another I saw a severed head given the full treatment with lip-stick, false eye-lashes and rouge: plus an ingenious brooch contrived from two ovaries and adjusted to lie against a neck-wrap of human tripe.

After the austerity of physiology, anatomy became an emotional release, if not a catharsis, and most demonstrators turned a blind eye.

I was no longer alone. Three friends made up an inseparable quartet and I am now the only survivor. Two died within sixteen years of graduation, and the third, a surgeon, George Arnott, after a professional life of only thirty-four years, so I had no difficulty in accepting a television announcement by a Glasgow University spokesman during 1972 that the *average* professional life of a male doctor was only twenty years. By 1972 the *average* professional life expectation for women was seven years owing to either marriage or death.

Our second degree professional examinations reduced numbers by more than a quarter. Failure in degree examinations was no anathema, one could sit again and yet again, though some, of course, left for greener grass elsewhere, but the Seconds were an important hurdle.

We all knew that the future meant live subjects instead of dead, and that we were probably now on the straight run to graduation. We worked when we felt like it and few lecturers felt so inadequate that attendances were compulsory.

These were years of do-it-yourself, painless learning which must be difficult for post-war unfortunates to appreciate, driven as they are towards examinations by threat of removal from the scene after a second examination failure in a major subject. We worked at our own speed, without compulsion, and because we were interested. We were proud to call ourselves 'students' and the world, more or less, approved us.

Hospital classes tended to be informal. Students tagged on to processions led round wards by a senior consultant, and inspected lumps, looked at X-ray plates from afar, listened to murmured words issued to sister or to juniors, occasionally touched flesh, and sometimes, very rarely, were able to test reflexes or listen to a heart.

My own first heart case was a girl of seventeen with mitral stenosis. Professor Harrington had decided to give his class a quick run through the technique of examination, and I became his victim. First, I was told, I must 'inspect' the chest and look for visible abnormalities. Since the girl was well stacked we all inspected eagerly.

We then passed on to 'palpation', which involved laying fingers or palm over the suspect area and attempting to sense various possible clinical signs. The professor was expecting me to detect a characteristic sensation which is imparted to the examining fingers and there is a special name, which he used. 'Any *thrill*?' He asked. The girl flushed and answered the question directed at myself. 'No, sir. Not with a boy of that age.' My goose was cooked, and it stayed cooked till someone else caught public imagination. I have told this story many times and heard it on television while completing this book! But it is true, and it is MY story.

Most patients were studied, when opportunity arose, with greater interest than if they had been giant pandas in the human zoo. None of us imagined that we, ourselves, might one day be patients, and we began to feel immortal. Thirty, we felt, was old, forty was senile, and fifty ripe for euthanasia . . . even then, a word occasionally used by philosophers (*sic*) in quiet rooms after their third or fourth whisky.

Gynaecology, we discovered, and very much to our surprise,

had nothing to do with sex. In fact, it switched everyone temporarily 'off' when we cut our teeth (so to speak) on the female pelvis in various out-patient clinics scattered throughout Glasgow. Turn-over was rapid and there was no nonsense about undressing in private, or nurses who looked like professional models ushering ladies on to agreeably designed couches. For most it was a case of skirts up, pants down, legs in the most embarrassing position possible and internal vaginal examinations, often without gloves. Thighs were usually grubby. Underwear often stank. Pubic hair could, on occasion, be lousy, and the situation killed all erotic notions. Slum vaginae, we discovered, were usually slack, polluted and foul. Now, almost forty years later, the scene has changed, and re-housing plus a fashion conscious world within the welfare state has created revolutions in personal hygiene. [Even if there is still some little way to go.]

Sir Robert Muir (Bobby to all who knew him) had the chair of pathology. He was a considerable scholar and top-flight scientist. He was also a craggy, lovable man and we met from time to time, long after I had been in practice and when he sensed change ahead and didn't like what he saw. 'Degrees don't make men,' he used to say. 'A man is only as big as his ability to meet situations. More wisdom and fewer degrees would make a better world.'

'Look after yourself, boy,' he growled during our last meeting. 'Newfangled ideas about medical education abound. They'll try to turn the universities into conveyor belts for blasted little yes-men and there won't be one giant in ten thousand. The sleekit bum-suckers will get into honours lists and rebels will have to leave the country. You'll see it happen. Medicine by machines is round the corner, and thank God I'm off elsewhere quite soon. But watch it, boy. Don't let them suppress you.' He died a few months later.

Bobby was the conscientious expert and far-seeing man of many parts. Carl Browning, in bacteriology, was the meticulous teacher and precisionist. Jointly, within their department, they did more than most to 'suggest' students into attitudes which became important.

Professor Harrington, who held the chair of medicine in Glasgow Royal Infirmary, was another giant, and memory of his belief in certain rock-firm rules saved a good many lives. The first, in particular, is all too often forgotten today when scientific gadgetry is supposed to be fool-proof. *But isn't!* Though not enough doctors appreciate that fact.

'A negative stomach X-ray isn't worth anything. Too many ulcers and early malignancies never show up. Surgeons never do wrong if they examine the belly in all chest cases and the heart in all suspect abdomens. Too many minor coronaries are laughed off as indigestion. If there's doubt about something inside an abdomen get a surgeon to open up and have a looksee. Remember that most patients are frightened. You'll not get far if you make them any more frightened. Don't bark or bite.'

A favourite surgeon was George Henry Edington of The Western. During early days I associated him with a hoity-toity senior staff less easy to understand than their more breezy colleagues in the Royal, but a chance meeting in the foyer during an interval of *Der Rosenkavalier* changed everything. The evening rounded off in his own home where I discovered he had firm ideas about what constituted an 'educated human being'. Courtesy, personal humility and personal integrity were taken for granted, but on top of that: 'a civilised and educated person should know his Classics, be able to give an informed criticism of any work of art, be conversant with contemporary literature and be able to appreciate not only good music, but good food, wine, and conversation in depth covering any topic of general interest. There is a trend towards super-specialisation. Ignore it. Concentrate upon becoming a cultivated man. After all, the human soul is more important than a W.1 office address or being the world's top authority on, for the sake of argument, the surgical treatment of ingrowing toe-nail.'

George Henry Edington was also the first tutor to use a four letter word about which no one in my experience knew anything whatsoever, since the 'soul' probably came within the orbit of Dr MacDonald, psychiatrist superintendent of Hawkhead Asylum, now Leverndale Hospital. Psychiatry was not particularly 'popular' in the middle thirties and Freud with Jüng made life complicated. In the beginning Doctor Mac reminded me of G. K. Chesterton, but after one visit to his home I saw him more as a John Buchan hero when he showed photographs taken of himself with the Mussolini family. They were all signed by Benito, and everyone was radiant. They gave me a new slant on the Italian dictator. The doctor was smiling. Benito was smiling. Edda was smiling. And it was difficult to understand how Doctor Mac could have become involved with such suspect company, because even by 1933–34 Mussolini had stopped being a comic opera buffoon. The doctor never explained his relationship, and although I saw him quite frequently he only smiled when I fished for clues.

'Yes, he was an interesting man.'

'No, he didn't look like starting trouble anywhere.'

'Sure, he was happily married.'

'Of course he liked Britain.'

Somewhere along the line Doctor MacDonald did something through this Mussolini contact to open a few imaginative doors for myself. How could acceptance by the Mussolini family reconcile with humdrum medicine in Glasgow?

John Glaister, professor of medical jurisprudence, was also a glamour boy scholar and his classes were among the most popular of all. He had been responsible for compiling Crown evidence in the Doctor Ruxton case when a family doctor had dismembered his wife and scattered fragments over various parts of Britain. The case had been complicated, and 'young John's' contribution was sensational. His book covering the affair was also sensational and excellent follow-up reading for those who used his equally splendid *Textbook on Medical Jurisprudence*. We all experienced what Sir John Frazer called 'the magic of contagion' when we were beside him, but I also began to understand that it would pay never to take quiet-looking, and apparently inoffensive gentlemen, for granted. 'Young John' was dapper, pale, with sleek and immaculately groomed hair, a small moustache and Dover Street-style clothes. He played everything in what is now called 'low profile' and it was difficult to appreciate exactly what drive and determination lay behind his cool public image.

Thinking back on these days I feel that the personality and achievements of our tutors were at least as important as their ability to teach. John Glaister, Sir Bobby Muir, Sir Donald MacAlistair, Tommy Bryce, George Henry Edington and others still to be mentioned had 'charisma' (for want of a better word) and, all unconscious, they instilled ideals which became more significant than their own subjects.

But Glasgow was also fortunate in having a covey of mighty obstetricians. This tradition may have begun years earlier with old Sir Hector Cameron, one-time Professor of Obstetrics and Gynaecology, who was succeeded by his son Sam. Sir Hector had no hesitation about keeping things in the family or seeing that his son got off to a good start even while a junior. His first lecture, I have been told, always began: 'Ladies and gentlemen. Books! You can buy this book on obstetrics or you can buy that book on obstetrics, but ye cannae dae better than buy oor Sam's.'

Memory of Sir Hector lived on for decades. Which is a long, long time by average standards in any average university. Nor did Sam let him down. I knew Sam best during his years of retirement when he had one main obsession, that he live long enough to make sure that each of his grandchildren was given a tailor-made shot-gun and rifle, without which, he often told me, no gentleman could hold his head up without blushing. Sam, in older age, had a jovial reddish purple face which crinkled into ready smiles. He wore tweeds and loved dogs, children, nature, guns, people and life itself. His enthusiasms were infectious.

My own obstetrics were soaked in through Professor Hendry, a genial character with a bark worse than his bite. I even took his class prizes, to the astonishment of all concerned, but he was, to some extent, overshadowed by two juniors – Dougal Baird, now Professor Sir Dougal Baird of Aberdeen, and Hector MacLennan, now Sir Hector MacLennan of Glasgow, of Scotland's National Tourist Board and goodness knows what else.

The young Dougal was sure, restrained, quietly self-confident, soft-spoken, lumbering and lucid, with many advanced ideas and a knack of being liked. He was, and is a man of compassion.

The young Hector was suave, smiling and affable, but so much like the actor Jack Buchanan that I often expected him to take a bow at the end of lectures or give an encore with '*Stand up and Sing*' (the hit of the moment). He was well-trained, vaguely patrician in his attitudes, a good teacher and beloved by his patients. It was unfair to say that this was due to his sex-appeal and Jack Buchanan personality. Even as students we knew that we were fortunate to have both Dougal and Hector around.

One comparatively junior teacher within another unit, however, was more radical and insisted on the wisdom of 'clamping' Fallopian tubes at the beginning of virtually any operation where the patient already had a large family and was either a Catholic or with a husband too stupid to be careful about contraception. It was also, in these days, easy to be so poor that it was impossible to buy contraceptives. He had even estimated the total number of births which had probably been prevented by this simple technique, and we were encouraged to ignore any philosophical arguments, but to concentrate upon the total spectrum of good which was likely to come from a very minor *temporary* interference.

It was bad luck that during very green cabbage days in London I did this to a mother of eight at the beginning of an appendicectomy, little knowing that my assistant was a devout Roman Catholic. He reported me, Gestapo-like, to the hospital superintendent, Murphy by name and also a Catholic. My first post-graduate confrontation with authority followed. No one was interested in my defence, an argument based upon knowledge that an ignorant and impoverished woman afflicted with six or seven more children than she could handle, and, nailed to a husband with no more consideration for his partner than a sex-starved gorilla in the zoo, did not wish any more children, or that her health might be seriously damaged if she again became pregnant. My forward-looking, if rebellious mentor's advice was, of course, illegal, even if it was sensible, apposite, reasonable and humane. I had never expected to meet the 'bum-sucking yes-men' predicted by Sir Robert Muir quite so early in my career! However, the world rolled on, and I was remanded, so to speak, on bail, with a warning 'not to do it again'. From then on I again watched 'Authority' with a wary and cynical eye.

Our obstetric course compelled us to confine twenty women 'on district' working with one other student only. This involved night trips through some of Glasgow's most sleazy territory and it should go on record that I never once saw a gang fight (except those provoked by students) and that I never even heard rumour of any student or nurse meeting with anything but total courtesy throughout Gorbals, Anderston, the Gallowgate, Ibrox, Cowcaddens or any other supposedly dangerous area.

George Arnott and I decided to get the 'district' thing over early in the term and we never paused to consider that we were going to confine girls before we had even completed the bookwork on how it was done.

An elderly 'howdy'* ran the district set-up in Glasgow's 'Rotten Row' Maternity Hospital (Rotten Row to everyone who knew it) and she was said to be ancient as sin itself. She was credited with being the only registered midwife in Britain to have been allowed to use forceps, and that when there was staff shortage during the First World War. She was small, brusque, immensely competent, capable of being 'motherly' towards timid students, but with a tongue which could have clipped steel. She watched Arnott and me report and did not seem to be impressed. 'Hae ye done any women before?'

'No, Sister.'

'Well listen to me. When ye get tae a hoose if the wummun is shoutin' "Mither! Mither!" look at her belly but come awa' back here. There'll be naethin' doing for hours. If she's screaming "Faither! Faither!" hold on a minute and make sure. She's maybe got less than a couple of hours. But if she's shrieking "Christ! Oh Christ!" then pit doon yer wee bag an' get ready for action. Now away with ye. Your first one's a multip of nine. She'll lay it easier than a hen does an egg.'

Her advice was sound. We applied it, and it worked like a charm. Sister MacDonald knew her stuff.

A partial (no doubt Freudian) blackout makes detail of these district evenings difficult to recall. Everything has been reduced to memories of gas-lit closes, puddles on pavements, shared dry privies, the smell of Dettol, beds built into inaccessible recesses, endless cups of tea, advice from husbands about sure-thing bets on dogs or horses, babies wriggling, plop, into a room warm with friendship and good neighbourliness, and the incomparably lovely noise of a new born infant's first cry. Tiny single end-rooms were usually clean enough. Even dirty flats had the

---

* Glaswegian patois=midwife.

confinement room in decent order. Patients knew that we were students, but they were grateful and always ready with a piece of slick repartee when it was all over.

Breast feeding was standard, and it is now my belief that no new housing estates will ever be tension free, until, somehow, the same natural sense of 'belonging' has been created which made so many of these tenement closes and dead end streets so securely cosy, in the same way that an Amazonian or Melanesian village is 'cosy' through observance of tribal law, sense of mutual dependence and sense of 'belonging'.

The so-called 'minor subjects' posed more problems at medical school than obstetrics, surgery or medicine. We all felt that they had merely been thrown in for good measure and I learned virtually nothing during classes on ophthalmology, oto-rhino-laryngology (ear, throat and nose), or dermatology, though one tutor in the 'skins' unit had a private jest which later figured in either *Penthouse*, *Playboy* or *Cosmopolitan*. The 'skins' clinic was in session for a semi-formal lecture when I heard it for the first time during the thirties. 'Tell me,' said the tutor, dead pan, 'what human organ is frequently soft but may become harder than bone, increases in length daily only to be reduced as occasion demands, which ladies prefer long, and gentlemen, on balance, prefer as more convenient, when short?'

He eyed the class and jumped for his kill on one girl who had begun to blush. 'You, there. I forget your name. What organ have you in mind?'

'The male reproductive organ, sir.'

The tutor looked at her impassively. 'If you believe that you are in for a disappointment. Harder than bone indeed. I refer, ladies and gentlemen, to the nails.'

The class tittered and life continued, but I often wonder where he first heard it. Such jokes usually have a long, long history.

Tragedy, thuggery, accident, attempted murder or suicide, broken limbs and razor slashes, tended, with a hundred other 'casualty' situations to reach The Gate of Glasgow Royal Infirmary, and The Gate was a hunting ground for 'experience'. On Saturday nights it could be a shambles, but it was also treasure trove for sensation-hunters. 'Casualties' arrived to take potluck. A comparatively senior surgeon was nominally in charge, but much responsibility was delegated to juniors doing a six-month stint, and for them the magic speedily wore off. Sheer pressure of work made willing hands welcome, and no questions were asked of anyone wearing a white coat who looked vaguely 'professional' – especially if he (or she) called all clearly senior persons 'sir' and did not annoy sister or the nursing staff.

During any typical winter Saturday night there might be five or six 'stunted' little 'gangsters' waiting for a head-stitching job. Few received sympathy and sutures could be, and often were, inserted by virtually anyone wearing that guarantee of respectability, the omnipresent white coat. One of my friends, a fourth year science man, dealt with more heads during one Saturday evening than the medical staff. Those little Neds were thin, pale, bandy-legged from rickets, almost illiterate, and in some cases speaking a dialect which was virtually incomprehensible. 'Worse than the Gaelic', said a divinity man while examining a woman with an incomplete abortion.

The Gate should have been engraved by Hogarth for posterity. I can so easily see what subjects he might have chosen. A drunk pissing into a kidney dish held by a teen-age junior nurse; that taxi-man digging fragments of glass from a lacerated hand while buxom Irish-lipped nurses held the blaspheming patient firm in his chair; or the tired-looking Doctor of Philosophy aesthete lazily wrapping a forearm in plaster while the patient bellowed abuse; a battered baby, with repentant mother standing beside a cot while three students worked over the father and kneed his crotch, hacked his shin, and filled his mouth with a thermometer to stifle screams; a baby, drunk from sugar lumps soaked in eau-de-Cologne – at that time an occasional West End, snob, infant 'comforter'; or a man fighting with two policemen in a corner after swigging a bottle of milk through which he had bubbled coal-gas . . . at that time the 'down-and-outs' cost-nothing passport to oblivion.

What a shambles, but what earthly paradise for the student body. Normally, of course, The Gate ran with decent efficiency, but on Saturday evenings and nights after football cup finals or Celtic v. Rangers matches it could be worse than chaos. Gate or no Gate, however, the Royal lived within a fading aura of distinction originally earned by Sir William MacEwan, who first evolved aseptic operating techniques and revolutionised hospital practice.

During the thirties the Royal was unpretentious, competent and conscious of its past, while the Western was said to be status conscious and more interested in the future. Deep in the South Side Glasgow's Victoria Infirmary quite unfairly rated as a cushy place for the second best. Which was rank injustice, since it, too, housed a quota of giants, among whom Norman Davidson, Robert Tennent and James Eric Paterson led the field. James Eric Pat was, indeed, one man of whom Glasgow should remain proud for a long long future. He was a pioneer in brain surgery in addition to being a general surgeon in local authority hospitals, and he owed Robert Tennent, who believed in his star, the fact that he had beds in the Victoria at all. But James Eric Pat chose to ignore the glamour potential of his speciality, and during years when Norman Dott of Edinburgh was stealing the headlines 'wee Pat' did his own thing in his own way, content in the knowledge that he was contributing within an almost unexplored field. I came to know him well. He was small, often acid, happy, humble, scholarly, and a faultless surgeon with wide interests. He did more to shape my own professional attitudes, surgical ability, character and long-term ambitions than any other person. His Victoria 'team' were also remarkable men. James P. Galloway, then assistant to Robert Tennent, usually assisted and Craig Borland was anaesthetist.

I first met them during my final year but saw Pat off and on until he died during the early sixties. Craig Borland became godfather to Craig, my first son, and James P. Galloway faded from our lives around the later fifties, but he was, at one time, my own idea of the perfect younger surgeon. He seemed to have everything – looks, personality, professional ability, character and wide general interests. He was ideal foil to Borland, who was small, pale, self-critical, professionally incorruptible, provocative in conversation and, even then, considerably learned.

Pat could be acid.

Jim Galloway was, in a sense, 'neutral'.

Borland was a catalyst who could induce conversation which, throughout several years, covered most of the human tragi-comedy. These talk sessions became more important to myself than even Pat's wizardry as a neurosurgeon or Jim's seemingly effortless ease in the general field. Few young people can have been so fortunate as I in being able to have a free seat during so many spectacular performances [even if none included a gastrectomy!].

Graduation was a mere formality. I already had roots in the Victoria and even deeper roots in our own local infirmary at Kilmarnock where I signed on to serve six months as house physician. I am now amused by one formality solemnly carried out before graduation when we all 'took' the Hippocratic Oath enjoining us to professional secrecy and God knows what else. I do know that almost every part of it was speedily broken, and that professional 'secrecy' became an old-hat idea which had, even by 1939, virtually gone by the board in many places throughout Britain.

Thinking back I also realise that these five undergraduate years were important because of extra-curricular activities which we could indulge without fear of being 'thrown out'. Failure in any degree examinations meant only explanations to parents who footed the total education bill. I played hard, but I also worked hard and I now know that play was important as any study routine, since life is an investment with broad portfolio and not for squandering on one obsession.

> Life's opening truth
> discouraged the youth
> but Instinct forced open
> a door.
>
> And the Goddess inside
> said: 'take me as a bride.
> I'm living, and Loving ...
> a whore.
>
> 'You'll pay me a price
> If you heed my advice.
> But when you die you'll remember
> Me well.

'Work without Me
is cursed, as you'll see.
If I'm jilted I'll show you
chill hell.

'I'm Serenity! Rich
discontentment! A Bitch!
Adventure! Nine Muses
in turn.

So bed Me and lay Me.
Conceive a life free.
Prove your way-deep-down passion
to learn.

'Take courage, young fool.
Do it My way and rule.
Don't wait, or you'll lose
foolish man.

'The happiness due
is given to few.
Just swyve me and don't give
a damn.'

I followed the advice of my subconscious and set out to
'conceive a life free' and 'swyve Fate' as commanded. It was a tall
order, but already I had changed beyond recognition in outlook. The depressions of earlier life were slowly being replaced
by the challenge of new ideas. Relationship with parents had
marginally improved, though I was far from even beginning to
understand them. More important, I had begun to laugh, to
laugh even at myself, and to feel a new confidence that the future
might, after all, be good. I had yet to learn that I had not really
come into contact with either illness or patients, but only looked
from afar upon impersonal situations which could not greatly
scar me. Perhaps I had allowed myself to be so taken up within
the broadness of living that medicine occupied only a very
peripheral part of life. If so, I had no complaints. Life had
become increasingly satisfying.

4 WASTING TIME PROFITABLY

There is much to be said for 'calculated waste of time'.

Conformists get no hang-ups from watching sunsets, listening to a lark, sniffing new mown hay, feeling a horse's muzzle or tasting wild strawberries. It is the possibility of other people watching sunsets while flirting with other sorts of bird, and rolling in the hay while nuzzling her muzzle or spearing a cherry which gets them down. And they cannot resist the Whitehousian compulsion to interfere.

The conforming do-gooder concept thumbs down polishing stage-door handles, study of the drug scene or contact with anything which is 'not quite nice'. Yet the same concept finds no time-waste in hob-nobbing with busy-body peers, status-symbolising or attempting to force personal views upon others, and it not only approves membership of the pollution club by usually driving unnecessarily large cars or organising multi-car households but is strangely silent about any obscenity which does not relate to sex.

Most of my tribe approved any experience which contributed to knowledge of what they believed to be 'good', but totally rejected contact with anything which their prejudices suggested was 'evil'. My elders predicted disaster, but I had a strong hunch that if life really was a one-way ticket on this planet it was only sensible to organise as many stop-overs as possible, and I welcomed those vague forces which were beginning to take over control as university life increasingly centred on The Union with its debates, high jinks, lectures and endless conversation.

Doctor Oliver H. Mavor, *alias* James Bridie the playwright, was also a consultant physician in Glasgow's Victoria Infirmary. But, said some, was it ethical for a distinguished physician to hob-nob with Bohemian types like actors, or, even worse, actresses. Small fry critics were also spreading the calumny that he would never write a good third act, so, since the jackals were snapping, it seemed to me to be a sure sign of ability. He was a good teacher, a likeable senior and a pillar of wisdom. One Mavorism has been passed on to countless patients. 'Never stand when you can sit. Never sit when you can lie, and never lie awake when you can lie asleep.' In other words, 'relax when possible'.

I seldom completed his 'advice', especially after the Welfare State got into full swing and when it became unnecessary to say: 'Never do today what you can get someone else to do for you tomorrow.' The nation found this out for itself as Welfare manna began to fall from social security offices, so I had no need to labour the point. Oliver Mavor was proof that a man need not be permanently anchored to his original profession, and living evidence that there is no justification for allowing life to direct one into a rut.

I also sensed real greatness in young John Barbirolli, who occasionally conducted Covent Garden at the Theatre Royal, and who held the baton for the Scottish Orchestra. I heard him conduct *Tristan* and returned in the same week to compare Beecham's approach to the same opera. Young Barbirolli, for my bet, had the edge on the *maestro*, though Sir Thomas may have been rattled by late arrivals who caused him to break off the overture and blast them for ill-manners. How many more times in the future was I to wish for a public figure of his stature who would use the same approach to those graceless boors who still arrive late in most British theatres.

Sir Thomas, young Barbirolli, and a mature Mavor projected impressions of technique in handling situations which were invaluable during eventual sultry sessions with awkward patients. Some responded to Beecham broadsides; others reacted better to acid Barbirolli-style barbs: a majority responded to mellow Mavorisms.

A few of D'Oyly Carte's Savoyards also projected impressions of long-term importance. Sir Henry Lytton's spark was fading when I watched him play Ko-Ko and shared coffee with him afterwards. Even on-stage he was then a sad little man with a cracked little voice, though still reflecting the magic which made him famous. Yet he was kind to a very junior person and reminisced happily about the 'old days', Gilbert's eccentricities, Sullivan's love of the sensuous, and the fatigue involved in long tours. This last seemed difficult to understand and it was only a score of years later, when I began to make my own one night stands, that I appreciated from lecture platforms just exactly how very kind he had really been in giving time to a stranger when he must have been longing to unwind. Memory made me more tolerant of others than might otherwise have been the case.

I also fell in love with Pitti-Sing, who was Marjorie Eyrie, and from time to time on until the middle forties met her and her husband, Leslie Rands, for an occasional meal and gossip. Leslie was my own favourite Savoyard, though never happy when singing the young poet in *Patience*. The jokes are 'corny' and he was convinced that he would forget his lines if ever Gilbert's little period jests failed to raise a laugh. He should have remembered that G. and S. audiences want the script exactly as it was written, but it was reassuring to know that even an expert could still, occasionally, lack a little self confidence.

Notions of romance were introduced into my strictly non-romantic, practical mind by Harry Welchman in both *The Desert Song* and *Casanova*. Harry was remarkably handsome and radiated charm. He was eclipsed only by Jack Buchanan, that man of impeccable distinction and stage wizardry. Jack had a chest complaint and occasionally stayed for shortish breaks in Arran where I met him from time to time, and from whom I learned much.

Stage people are more generous, *sympatique* and self-critical than most members of orthodox professions, and even at college I was asking myself what happened to 'secure' people who play life 'safe' and opt into the retire-with-a-pension routine. Too often something seems to die inside, and they become afraid to live. So I began to learn, at quite an early age, the basis for advice which has been handed out throughout most of my life from every possible platform.

Security kills something 'inside'.

Life is for living.

Try anything once. Including vice.

Retire and die.

Pension schemes work because contributors don't live to draw upon them.

Don't wait till next year. Tomorrow may never come.

Clothes don't make the man, but they affect how he feels.

'Ambition' is the greatest killer, 'Fame' the greatest aphrodisiac.

Tell your wife you love her, even if it chokes you.

It is easier to adapt to rising than to adjust after a fall.

Mediocrities make little-big-men feel good.

The most important status symbol is to be so well adjusted that you feel no need for status symbols.

Aphorisms, wise cracks and epigrams, sparkled out from conversations in places ranging from the Union coffee-lounge to city offices on Saturday mornings where secretaries were usually able to take life easily since the boss-men seldom appeared, and, like models from the Art School, they appreciated the company of students.

Knowledge sometimes came from unexpected people, and when the Prince of Wales chartered the yacht *Nahlin* from Lady Yule in order to sail with the then Mrs Wallace Simpson down the Adriatic coast, one of the stewards was an Ayrshire acquaintance, who also taught me an important lesson. 'Work' he said was 'bloody non-stop.' Shore leave, I gathered, was rare, but a night ashore had been promised for Dubrovnik (then Ragusa). Last minute cancellation was said to be due to Mrs Simpson organising an unexpected party, and, my acquaintance said grimly that he hoped they enjoyed it 'because the lads spat on every sandwich while it was being made. Pâté and spittle,' he added. 'Or maybe cucumber and a snort, since one of the lads 'ad a cough.'

This small piece of history has not, to date, figured in the Windsor story! My only justifications for mentioning it now are to show how the improbable does happen, and how wise it is not to cross kitchen staff or ships' stewards, who have an answer for everything. My own first cruise on board the *City of Nagpur* cost, in 1934, thirteen pounds for a fourteen day round trip including Corunna, Lisbon, Cadiz, Madeira, Las Palmas and Casablanca, each of which did something to an inquisitive mind.

'The Compound' in Casablanca was, at that time, a village within a city, surrounded by high walls and encaging only criminals. It was a sort of limboland for outcasts. There was no rule of law inside and visits could be a hairy experience. I was with John Kerr, due on the following year to graduate First Class Honours in Chemistry and to be the most distinguished student of his year: but we left at speed, chased by an enraged mob of multi-caste girls dressed only in pale turquoise butter-muslin mini-frocks. Trouble arose because they caught two greenhorns off-guard and not knowing that their only way to meet the situation was to choose a girl and pay for the experience. Built-in prudery, some shock and acute shortage of cash made us decide instead to run. The pack was gaining when we reached a gate, and a hail of stones spattered round us as we piled into a taxi. Visits in later years were less exciting but suggested an increasing interest in what Craig Borland has described as the 'incomparable appeal of low life'.

I fell in love with *Fado* in Lisbon, drank hundred-year-old wine in Funchal, brooded about getting engaged in Las Palmas to a honey-coloured damsel wearing ankle length mantilla, and attended High Mass in Cadiz Cathedral. The trip was a roaring success and I fell in love with ships, learned to listen to seamen's jokes, discovered how middle-aged men tend to have a flutter with teen-age females, and proved that ships' Masters represent God, the monarch and the country only when on their own bridge and at sea, a knowledge it was useful to apply when, in due course, I made voyages as a member of the lecture panel for P and O Lines cruise-ships between 1962 and 1972. In fact, it has been odd how early experiences at university and during cabbage years paid long-term dividends in unexpected places decades later.

Every moment was invested and who, I now keep asking, can dare to judge what is 'waste'? Every personality who crossed my bows also contributed something, though G. K. Chesterton was a disappointment. I found him pretentious, forcedly jocular and trying too hard. Perhaps he was having an off day! John Buchan, Lord Tweedsmuir as he then was, proved better value for money. He was cool, but not too cool, though with the tense face of a potential duodenal ulcer. His humour was gentle, modest, quizzical and charming. I do not remember one single thing he said, but I do know that he, too, again underlined a point which interested me. Harry Lauder's *Road through life* was

44

not the shortest distance between two points. It could be zig-zagged indefinitely.

Sir Harry Lauder himself lived not so far from either Glasgow or Kilmarnock and I cannot think of any artist today who would get away with what he did to his audiences. He eventually tended to change his kilt between every song. But he was old, and the rest may have been essential. Several years after his death I approached his niece, Gretta, at Lauder Ha' to see if she would allow me to write his biography. 'Listen, son,' she said at last. 'I've had Irving Berlin on his knees in front of me asking to do uncle's life. But I said "Irving. The time isn't ripe. I'll let you know when I make up my mind".' Sadly she never did make up her mind, and now she, too, has gone. The Hall was sold up and Danny Kaye beat me at the auction for a Lauder walking stick which I wished to buy. The definitive biography still needs to be written.

The Lauder scene puzzled me because I knew that the Scot he projected did not exist, and probably never had existed. It was a caricature drawn from a synthesis of Glasgow-Lanarkshire lower working-class slums presented in a phoney national dress and endowed with over-stated qualities of meanness, pawky humour, humanity, courage, shrewd logic and back-street repartee. Lauder's Scot had the wisdom of Solomon, the sentimentality of Victorian Christmas cards, the humour of a spring-cleaned Edwardian music-hall comedian, the courage of Gorbals die-hards, the charm of sheer simplicity, and the hard-headed shrewdness of a French peasant. It is little wonder that Scots adored him. The great, big, little-man made them walk tall, though the fact remains that his Scot was a fantasy. It took me years to appreciate exactly why he did appeal so deeply deep down to a race which pretends to pride itself on despising sentiment.

During our Fourth Year, George Arnott, and a friend Jack Shields, later Medical Officer of Health for Kirkcudbrightshire, organised a four week motoring tour through France and Spain. The car was a Morris 'eight' and the scene on every level was vastly different from today, but the trip taught me plenty about the human comedy. We first discovered, in San Sebastian, how cold tea can be passed off as whisky by bar-girls working for the house. An irritated waiter who drew a knife when I disputed a late-night bill in Madrid also proved exactly how it feels to have cold steel touching bare skin over the gall-bladder area. I saw crates of guns and cartridges stored within the closed crypt of Toledo cathedral and was thrown out by an excited priest who would, no doubt, have been shot several months later when all but one of the Toledan clergy were slaughtered within the bull-ring.

Few roads were sealed, and it was four bumpy hours from Madrid to Toledo, while the run from Valencia to Gerona took almost four days and broke two springs. Torremolinos was a sleepy village and Marbella a negligible hamlet. Benidorm and Calpe could have been bought for a few thousand pounds. Sitges was a dusty seaside semi-slum and Barcelona ripe for war as splinter political groups planned murder in side streets around the Ramblas. Machine-guns and civil-guards were posted on Plaza di Cataluña. Bandits hung around occasional valleys reaching towards the Pyrenees, and some of these continued even after the Civil War right up until 1953 when a British doctor was shot dead during an ambush on a route south from Andorra shortly before I took my own young family along the same road.

I was also fortunate in making a first visit to the old Bal Tabarin on a night when Parisians were dancing in the streets. *Le can-can* was *the* Tabarin speciality and *les girls* gave it the full treatment. Any *can-can* in any other place has always been a pale imitation.

I also began to wonder about the Mona Lisa and to question expert opinion. I still wonder, and I still do. Restorations, time, colour-changes and titivating, have made her, by my assessment, look like a woman with bad teeth and a low I.Q.

Total cost was £23 – an interesting proof of what 'inflation' has meant since the war. The trip also underlined thoughts which were sliding into focus. There is no credit due to virtue acquired through life in an ivory tower, or as flaunted by people who have never been exposed to temptation.

So 'temptation' became important.

How could I know what sort of person I was way down inside unless I knew how I would react to every situation possible?

How could I criticise others if I didn't know, through personal experience, my own reaction to what my elders called 'sin'? How could I give relevant advice about anything unless I could speak at first hand? Tribal Organisation placed a high value on external evidence of 'goodness' and apparent respectability, but I was more interested in self-awareness, in discovering my own hang-ups and in the creature 'inside'.

Student life had already taught me that most people wore a mask.

How did they react behind it?

Was it likely that 'they' would react in broadly the same way as myself to any given situation, since we were basically the same tribal creatures? Or were we?

Could I discover clues as to how problems affected others by exposing my own life to temptation on all fronts? And if so would I have character enough to avoid disaster? Would the experience help me to be a better human being or a better medicine man?

I figured that it would. And I figure that it did. Indeed, so strongly do my wife and I feel about letting youth flex its muscles that our own two boys have been encouraged to pass longish times in unusual places as one method for getting their priorities nicely organised right from the beginning.

Freedom *may* be dangerous, but unreasonable discipline, in my experience, is more so. Though my own first taste of freedom in London, when I was nineteen and completely alone, became complicated. We were having a summer in Upminster so that Alistair might benefit from a better climate, when I met an Italian who invited me to afternoon tea in his suite. He proved to be a homosexual, a condition about which I then knew less than nothing, and I reacted violently. But the violence also taught me a lesson, because I only hit him once, and he was knocked unconscious. I realised that I must not, ever again, strike a person in fear or anger. I even became a little afraid of my own strength, but I left the suite quietly and walked with as much nonchalance as I could muster away from the hotel. We had met, originally, over luncheon at a shared table when conversation was stimulating and I was flattered that such a mature man could show real interest in myself. A visit to the British

47

Museum followed, and his later invitation to see a miniature bought on the previous day seemed reasonable. But the experience surprised me.

Shortage of money also made me brood about stealing. I discarded the idea, but it left me sympathetic to several patients who went the whole hog and landed in sorrow. Had the same temptation not come my own way years earlier I might have handled their affairs differently. As it was, I worked hard to save them from arrest, and persuaded employers to settle for repayment of money over a period of time. In one case the sum was heavy and would normally have carried a prison sentence.

Five shillings (twenty-five pence today) could, in these days, buy fish with chips, toast and a pot of tea for two; a quarter pound of chocolates and admission for two to decent seats in the cinema. Charity Day rags collected enough addresses of agreeable girls to see most of the student body through until the next year, so five shillings tended to be spent every Friday night. My parents were happy enough about returning home late on Fridays since they had accepted the lie that medical students 'were supposed to hang about the wards to see what came in', but this was wearing thin by the end of the fourth year, and rumours linking me with a girl called Kathleen MacLelland, who served in Smith's Wool Shop, unexpectedly reached H.Q. in Kilmarnock. The family, to my surprise, decided to play things cool and finally let matters slide after several scouting expeditions by my mother, who said that she was a 'sensible looking girl and that there would be no objections to my seeing her from time to time, provided we never sat in the back of my car together'.

Kathleen was, in fact, an attractive property, good company, a good dancer with a flair for clothes, a sense of humour and a rather dead-pan serenity which I found appealing. My wife and I met her again about fifteen years later when she had nicely settled into family life in Uddingston. It was probably an all-round traumatic experience. She had changed and I had changed. Trudie, my wife, studied her with interest while her husband watched me with what looked like grave suspicion, and the visit was not repeated. The moral seemed clear! Even so, Kathleen was part of my extra-curricular life at Medical School and I began to appreciate those temptations which had cost my parents sleepless nights in earlier days. It follows that I welcomed the blast of change which hit the country during the later sixties. What a breed of hopeless cowards most of us were in the old days!

During my whole medical course I received no instruction worth listening to about the one problem which was most likely to occupy time if, when I became a family doctor, I was prepared to involve myself with the *cause* of patients' headaches, skin rashes, quarrels, ulcers, blood pressures or frustrations as opposed to *treating them symptomatically*.

One particular lecturer skimmed round the shadow of the periphery of the subject while coping with Public Health. He looked uncomfortable, and probably felt uncomfortable, but the class was agog for practical advice and worth-while sex education. We were all in a receptive mood and wanted to *know*. Instead, he leaned across his lectern and said something like this, according to my notes. 'Sex is odd. Strange! But some men will even pay a woman five pounds just for half-an-hour in a taxi. Reprehensible! Sort of thing which spreads venereal disease and makes public health work so much more difficult!'

We left more puzzled than when we came in, but I now believe that he said nothing because he knew nothing. The idea of equating pleasure with sex (especially in a taxi) was anathema to university Organisation right up until long after the Second World War. Little wonder that most doctors, and virtually all nurses, were unable to cope with sex problems, and that any patient asking for practical advice wasn't likely to get very far. Home, school, church, university, press and government alike seemed determined to repress even the most elementary suggestion that sex knowledge might promote spiritual contentment.

It has been easy for me to understand why so many parents of my own generation, and even younger, have lately been jealous of their own children and of the freedoms which they have won. Some have actually used the word 'jealous' when involved in patient relationships with myself, yet these, as a rule, have been among the parents most vicious in their public damnation of sex, even within their own family.

Medical Jurisprudence introduced the police courts and I listened to a young John Cameron both defend and lead for the Crown. I also heard Mr Justice Avory, an ascetic person of Olympian dignity, condemn men to death during years when judges uttered sentence from under the black cap. No man whom I saw doomed in the old style reacted, and warders told me that they often met the hangman with equal impassivity.

The High Court also taught me how tense drama can be presented in very low key and interest in the scene has never worn off, though, by my own estimate, few judges have so graced a bench as did that same young John when he became Lord Cameron.

On balance I neither approved nor disapproved of capital punishment. It was a feature of life like examinations, climate, income tax, fog or threat of war, but after thirty years in medicine I now have the half-formed impression that there is something to be said for reviving the death sentence, at least for selected cases including poisoners and murderers of policemen, child rapists, drug pushers and aircraft hi-jackers.

After confirming that I had 'satisfied the examiners' I made a swift trip to Poland before graduation in 1936. An uncle, Bob Howie, had certain contacts among Scandinavian royalty, and I met a Crown Prince in his London office before leaving. He instructed his consul in Danzig to look after me, and I arrived to face an off-beat routine.

Hitler and the Nazis were active and take-over was all but complete. Prince August was, I think, number 35 in the Party, and later executed after the abortive anti-Hitler bomb plot, but he was then in Danzig with a delegation including several men who were eventually hanged at Nürnberg. An immense parade had been organised around Saint Mary's Platz and I was fortunate in sitting among the top brass with my consul host only a few paces away from where the Prince took the salute. Scores of thousands marched past that afternoon, yet the man's forearm never quivered, and he stood, rock firm, in full Nazi rig, for longer than I would have thought possible. The goose-step clanging of boots against cobbles re-echoed in memory for years. The Platz, that afternoon, was overlaid by an aura of evil, and I sensed for the very first time that there were sins more bizarre in this world than the limited imagination of my sub-tribe could conceive. Mass hysteria was also close to the surface, and although the Nazi drama had still to be fully revealed enough had happened to point the future. I met all these men after the parade in the world famous liqueur house called Sachs, where free Güld-Wasser was one of the burgomeisters' perks of office. The liqueur was water-clear and sticky but with fragments of what looked like gold leaf floating inside. A few years later most of the Sachs family were murdered by the Nazis for refusing to reveal the secret of their house-drink – though who could have guessed what lay ahead when we all stood together in the timbered rooms of that gracious old home and toasted one another with gold-water? The Nazis were anxious, at that time, to be civil towards even an unimportant British student, given that there was a possibility he might return home with good reportage. Nor had they forgotten that certain English students, in a historic Union debate, had voted against fighting for 'king and country'.

As a student I seemed to be more significant to top brass Nazis and a ci-devant prince in Danzig than I was in my own home town, which was both amusing and thought-provoking. During the short return voyage to London I remembered Doctor MacDonald of Hawkhead and his friendship with the Musso-linis. Perhaps, I thought, some of these doors were not so difficult to open after all.

A few days later Destiny applied my nose to a gritty grind-stone inside Kilmarnock Infirmary.

My salary was £2 per week . . . more or less.

Board was supplied, but the quality was bad.

Bed was hard, though seldom used for more than a few hours on end, and half days were possible only by arrangement with colleagues. Which meant that they could be forgotten: what one gained on the swings one lost on the roundabouts. A few hours 'off' at most was all that was practicable. Holiday leave, of course, was nil, unless a locum was provided and paid for by the house officer.

Hours on duty worked out at twenty-four per day: enjoy-ment potential was minimal: experience potential was good: opportunity for tension was unlimited, since, like all other

51

house officers, fatigue took over at an early date. That apart, we had to assume a preposterous amount of responsibility – responsibility, in fact, which is now accepted only by trained biochemists, pathologists, blood-transfusion experts and the like. Given that one had any conscience at all I had to consider, right from the beginning, whether I was really equipped to cope, and whether I was morally entitled to perform duties about which I had had no conception when accepting the post.

All in all, I still believe that this six month stretch caused irreparable damage to body and mind. After one early day of desperate problems I even dreamed about Aesculapius, and listened to his sacred snake give strange advice.

> The serpent slipped slowly down from its staff
> and said 'let the Play begin
> while The Harpies scream, with cackling laugh,
> "*We'll* win. We know *we'll* win".
>
> 'Show them your guts and prove them wrong.
> They're psycho, crazy mad.
> But the world goes along with their weirdy song,
> not bad, my boy, just mad.
>
> 'Though a few find Truth, and walk alone
> with the Goddess hand in hand.
> So give Her your life, and stifle that moan,
> She may teach you to understand
>
> 'that the world is ruled by fops and fools
> bluffing or playing by ear,
> while they help each other to break the rules
> as mediocrities cheer.
>
> 'What is Wisdom, Truth or Soul?
> "Philosophers' Barbs," they say,
> and continue to score self-interest's goal.
> Weaklings drifting astray.
>
> 'Cheating to live! Afraid to die!
> Phoney, pathetic small men
> keep passing the buck, scared to say "why",
> or "Hi! Will you please explain?"'

The snake wriggled gently back into place
his last words searing my mind:
'Let your weapons be honesty – charity – truth.
Be faithful – hopeful – be kind.'

Philosophers have often enquired about the stuff of which dreams are made. But could this really have been a dream? Can a dream end by leaving the dreamer with a complete poem, and a message which did, after moments of stress, compose a mind which way deep down was still lonely? The poem lay among my more personal papers for thirty years before I decided to have it published in this book, and for thirty years it served, from time to time, to remind me of mysteries which had first been suggested on that magical afternoon years earlier when I found my fairy. At lowest estimate the 'dream' was a supranormal experience which left me with a written 'message' and advice which I tried, throughout life, to put into practice.

But it did more, because one must remember how, at that stage of life, I was supposed to be a thoroughly indoctrinated Christian, and for certain I knew nothing of older faiths which extended back to what Australian aborigines call 'before Dreamland'. Yet the 'dream' suggests personal contact with a messenger from another level of development and even mentions The Goddess. Some might say that it was even written from analeptic memory. Others, more 'practical' explain it as subconscious memories from childhood · reading being blended, through stress, into a message which is really nothing more or less than standard Christian teaching . . . at least in the last verse. But there is more to the poem than a last verse and the content is far more mature than could be expected from a 'normal' twenty-three-year-old man. If it did nothing else the poem gave me a curious hope and sense of belonging . . . to Somebody. I hoped that one day I would find out more.

5 HOW *NOT* TO DO ALMOST EVERYTHING, YET SURVIVE

I was no stranger to Kilmarnock Infirmary. Our family doctor, John William Peden, was also visiting surgeon, and during my last three years at medical school I had pottered about his unit. His partner, George Currie, a visiting physician, allowed the same freedom, and the place became a home from home. Thinking back, it seems odd that I never appreciated how much was expected of the resident medical staff.

Peden was a jovial character, an ideal family doctor, conscientious, competent, reassuring and wise. He had been trained under Sir William MacEwen, one of the all-time maestros, and I learned much surgery only one hand-shake away from the cream of the cream. George Currie, however, was a different kettle of fish and a neutral-grey sort of person. First clash with Authority unexpectedly developed one late evening when need arose to carry out a blood transfusion in an attempt to save the life of a novice from nearby Nazareth House. I telephoned the Mother Superior and explained the situation. She agreed that a blood donor would have to be found and arranged to send down 'some people' for typing.

I was taken aback, after such a promising beginning, when six or seven unhappy children arrived shortly afterwards in care of a young nun who explained that they were volunteer donors. She was not impressed when I rejected them as unsuitable. On balance, I felt that they would all have reacted well to a couple of pints themselves. 'Where,' I asked, 'could I find a young and healthy adult nun?' Telephone conversations with Nazareth House became acid on both sides and final discussion with the Mother Superior ended on a high note of mutual criticism. Two or three youngish nuns did, however, finally arrive and I got down to the (then) tricky task of typing their blood groups. Since I had never done this before, and had learned only the theory of the business, only a rash man would have accepted any of the conclusions.

Fear, irritation, personal uncertainty, and knowledge of my own incompetence made me rash, though the devil (or someone) looked after his own and I did select a type known at that time as a 'universal donor'. (Events proved that my 'typing' efforts had been accurate – though some days passed before I was completely reassured, but, since she recovered, all must have been well.)

The technique for 'direct cross-typing' was way beyond my resources, even when spurred on by desperation.

When the 'universal donor' discovered that she was 'suitable' she reached a moment of truth and refused to co-operate. Only direct intervention from her superior eventually made her a reluctant victim but the various confrontations involved had also, by then, made me an uncertain junior house physician, and I made a mess of the whole business.

The idea was to use a large syringe with a three-way cock and with needles into the vein of donor, recipient, plus a bottle of sodium citrate solution to reduce risk of clotting. Technique was: close taps to donor and patient; open tap communicating with citrate and withdraw 1 or 2 ccs; close tap: open donor tap and withdraw 20 ccs of blood; close donor tap; open patient's tap and inject blood plus sodium citrate into the vein. Repeat the cycles.

It sounds complicated even to read! It was even more complicated to do, especially since the patient's veins were so collapsed that blood refused to flow. I then used a local anaesthetic on the front of the patient's arm, cut down on a vein, slit it gently open, and replaced the needle with a glass cannula. By that time the needle in the donor's arm was blocked with clotted blood and my connection into the citrate did not look so good either. Nor did I work alone! One or two curious nuns had joined the group of spectators, having been admitted by an Irish sister whose majestically aggressive personality would not be denied. One or two other nurses were also around, since 'doing a blood transfusion' was more or less equivalent in publicity value during 1936 to transplanting a heart in 1972. I once thought that I also glimpsed a black dog, but that was either a materialised hound from hell or a product of my deranged imagination.

Five hours later and four pounds lighter in weight, I finally wrapped the thing up, ordered coffee and decided that there would never be a 'next time' – at least, not before the Infirmary got itself some more suitable equipment. My instructions to the nurses who assisted me had begun to sound like an Aristophanes conversation in the agora. 'Close recipient's tap: shut yours Sister . . . a drop more of the real MacKay you silly girl . . . close that bloody tap woman and open mine . . . I mean hers . . . damn it, you know what I mean . . . and I didn't bloody swear either . . . close your tap . . . tap, woman . . . Not trap . . . I wasn't being offensive . . . If I want to be offensive you'll bloody know it . . . See, you stupid cow, hold my cock . . . Jesus wept, girl . . . the patient's cock . . . Nurse, there's blood dribbling all over the place . . . close the tap, girl. Close.'

The following day was eventful. Senior staff heard garbled stories from our local gestapo which operated along lines similar to Stalin's NKVD.

The Hospital Secretary heard about it on a more official level from Nazareth House and was not amused.

The Hospital Board heard about it from the Hospital Secretary.

The Matron early heard about it from the Irish sister.

A local Church of Scotland minister heard about it from the Matron.

My parents heard about it from the minister, from myself, from George Arnott and from various untraced sources.

I became either famous, infamous, eccentric, reliable, unreliable, anti-Catholic, arrogant or too self-confident according to the point of view, and tempers were only beginning to cool off when Fate dealt me a second scurvy trick which settled all doubts.

Yet the incident was over within a few minutes.

A youngish nurse had rushed out of a ward in a state of what looked like near hysteria and caught me in a corridor. A woman had aborted towards the end of her third month. She had done so during the ward's bed-pan session. An Irish nurse had told a priest who had just finished administering extreme unction to a man dying in the private room of another ward. The priest had then 'forced' his way into the female ward 'while all the women

56

were on their bed-pans' and insisted on 'performing a service' over the foetus. Sister had then sent the nurse to find a doctor and get him to put the priest out of the ward.

Thinking back, there was a sort of cumulative hypnotic effect about the whole business. The nurse's distress got me bothered. My prudish upbringing told me that it was improper for a man to be around during the bed-pan routine (doctors excepted, of course, but even they only during an emergency). Probably subconscious hostility towards any member of the organisation which had raised such botheration over my blood transfusion incident also made me relish an attack, knowing that this time virtue was on my side. Most of all, the fact that sister had sent a nurse to fetch a doctor to eject the priest registered a big hit. In hospital, at that time, junior house officers did exactly what sister wanted, and when and how she wanted it. And with no argument.

Sadly, the priest failed to see my point of view.

The scene is engraved in memory for ever, but it can be left to the imagination of others to fill in details. A mostly naked fat woman was still lying on a pool of blood beside a tiny foetus mixed up with clot and two white-faced nurses were frozen into immobility as the little man in black did his thing while his small appurtenances of office lay around. These were the head-lines.

A furious priest then demanded to know by what right he was being interrupted. Taking it from there the immediate drama was swiftly transferred to the corridor outside the ward where it had all begun, and since local citizens were collecting for visiting hour due to begin a few moments later it can be understood that there was no shortage of witnesses. We were interrupted only by sister rushing along to say that the ward was now clear and that 'Father could go in again', a development which bought a little time and enabled me to sum up the future.

On balance, I decided that I would be fired. I also appreciated that I had been thrown in at the deep end of very big business affecting a chum-club which had a larger-than-usual membership. So I was bound to lose. But I had reckoned without the wheels within wheels, and after a day or two of behind-the-scenes discussion I heard that all was forgiven. At the same time, either George Currie or John Willie Peden suggested need for future discretion, and beyond a mildly avuncular ticking off all was well – except that I had earned a totally unjustified reputation for being 'anti-Catholic'.

The days passed in non-stop work. Patients admitted during the night had to have their case-reports written up in detail for arrival of Doctor Currie at around nine ack emma, by which time all relevant 'tests' had to be carried out. This usually meant 'blood counts' which should, in my view, only be handled, as they are now, by trained technicians, and I was no trained technician. If there was suspicion of diabetes a blood sugar estimate might also have to be done. Complete urinalysis was standard procedure and if there was any question of suspect kidney function a blood urea might also be tackled during the night. Many years have passed since house officers have been expected to do this sort of work, which properly belongs to the biochemists or pathologists. When added to routine clerking, ward rounds, night rounds, dealing with emergencies, supervising various types of treatment, carrying out lumbar punctures or respectfully drinking coffee after ward rounds with chiefs or sub-chiefs (all local general practitioners) no day had enough hours. That apart, battles with conscience generated even more tension which sometimes found outlets through unexpected channels, as when Arnott and I became involved in dispute with kitchen staff and hospital secretary over both quantity and quality of food!

To say the least of it, the stuff was dreadful. Catering was supervised by the Matron, a lady of generous proportions physically and, in my view, limited proportions in many other respects. She was one of those girls of the old brigade who tended to begin sentences with: 'what would dear Miss Nightingale say?' And it was time wasted to suggest that Miss Nightingale, having been far ahead of her own time, and given that she was on form, would probably have said a great deal. Even with a different slant from what Matron and others of her ilk implied!

Eventually, and in desperation, we made arrangements for lunch to be sent up by a local caterer. The effect of this upon the Hospital Secretary was remarkable. We were refused the right to have food sent in to the hospital even when we paid for it ourselves. Our actions were 'disloyal' (that sinister word which usually comes out only when authority is unable to produce any other argument). We were ungrateful young pipsqueaks (a period word), and we were instructed to cancel the orders forthwith.

This extraordinary situation led to a meeting with Matron in her capacity as kitchen Poo-Ba; with the senior cooks, mostly graduates from the 'Dough School' (more respectfully known as the Glasgow and West of Scotland School of Domestic Science); and with the Hospital Secretary representing the lay administration. Matters were not improved when George Arnott said that the high incidence of duodenal ulcer in the West of Scotland was probably due to the Dough School if what we had been having was a sample of the best it could do.

Apologies all round: reluctant from the house-officers, vague from the Matron, threatening from the Secretary and tearful from the young cooks, led to a temporary improvement in our board.

It was just unfortunate that I was laid very low with 'jaundice' only a short time later! The Secretary, Matron and cooks seemed to take this as a deliberate affront to prove some point I had never even implied about cleanliness in the kitchens. Arnott thought it funny until he found himself obliged to do my own work, after which it stopped being even vaguely amusing, and he did not rest until my chief had arranged for a locum to cover my own duties.

Meanwhile, I was given the conventional perquisite of office and laid up in a 'side-room' (now called an amenity-room) for just under four weeks. I returned to duty jaded, with no appetite and still pasty-yellow around the eyes, but was shortly afterwards bowled over by receiving a bill from the Infirmary which exceeded my total six month earnings. It seemed that, contrary to all medical tradition, I was going to be soaked locum salary for the period of my absence plus standard rates for use of a 'private room' – which I had not requested and which, in any case, was a traditional perk of office at that time.

There was only one thing to do. The house officers gave official notice to the Management committee that if the bill was not withdrawn we would walk out on the following morning. I also took time off to see Lord Rowallan, Chairman of the Board, and explained the situation. He was understanding, sensible and constructive and I left feeling that something would be done about it, though George Currie was less encouraging. I figured that I would be foolish to rely on his vote and concentrated attention upon the Secretary, with whom we now had a worthwhile love-hate relationship.

I was eventually taught the importance of 'compromise', that word beloved by all 'grey' people.

An emergency meeting decided to cancel fees for my private room, but one from whom I was entitled to expect support, is said to have insisted that I pay for my own locum. The locum rates were far above what I earned and final decision was an extraordinary departure from tradition. I emerged from that episode with the label anti-establishment round my neck to balance the anti-Catholic one earned a month or so earlier. Thereafter I seldom trusted any man in a position of authority to support a junior in any dispute with any Organisation. It was a useful philosophy to acquire at the beginning of any professional life and has long stood me in good stead.

My father's advice became understandable. 'You'll never be happy until you can look any man in the eye and tell him to go to hell without worrying about the consequences.'

Somehow it was apt that an incident involving my blood pressure should suddenly blow up at around this stage in time. George Currie had acquired a new toy. It registered blood pressure and pulse rate on a graph and I was used as guinea-pig while he got the hang of it. When the first roll of paper ran off the line he looked at it with interest, glanced at me curiously, and said that my blood pressure was so high I would not live to be forty.

An irreversible neurosis was born in that same second from a remark which was unforgivably stupid and professionally improper. With it was also born my own determination never to make remarks to patients which would cause tension as I remembered Professor Harrington's advice: 'most patients are scared. You won't get far if you make them any more scared': and I felt sick.

The curious thing is that I actually believed what the man

said. A few months later I visited Doctor Joey Wright, then senior assistant to Professor Harrington, and told him the story. He checked my pressure and was reassuring. Yet I did not believe him. I now realise that it was useful to go through this sort of emotional upheaval right at the very beginning of my professional career, because I had accepted the spontaneous remark of a big-mouth junior physician, yet rejected the definitive diagnosis of an expert, suspicious that he might only be lulling me into a false sense of security. How many patients have done the same thing? My own adventure taught me to be sympathetic where, otherwise, I might well have been irritated.

Since that day no one has been able to take an accurate reading of my blood pressure. Consolation lies in the fact that at 58 my best recent reading is much the same as my best reading at 23, and my heart tracings are said to be normal.

I did learn, however, at least for a few months, how it might feel to know that life would be short, so I decided to make it very, very sweet and began to burn the candle at both ends. In spite of work-load Arnott and I shared time-off to the limit and I averaged about four hours nightly in bed for the last two months in Kilmarnock. Daughters of family friends were husband-hunting and having twenty-first birthday parties all over the county, or else dancing cheek-to-cheek at most lush hotels between Loch Lomondside and Ayr. I also smacked a golf ball to get rid of aggressions, while the theatre took up every 'spare' evening and I even turned down one offer of marriage. The girl had inherited sixty thousand pounds, was said to be 'a push-over' and was crazy about ballet. She switched me off chiefly because she enjoyed telling dirty stories and wanted me to grow a beard.

Kilmarnock ended without regret and I returned to Glasgow Victoria as house surgeon under Robert Tennent and James Galloway. My friend 'wee Pat' was still doing his neuro-surgery and Craig Borland coping with many anaesthetics. The atmosphere was civilised, agreeable and work sensibly supervised. I was even encouraged to do a little research into an 'original idea' and worked up a thesis bearing upon blood iodine levels in thyrotoxicosis. The work continued for a further year and led to my Doctorate of Medicine in 1939.

To some extent I had been prepared for work under Robert Tennent after spectating for three years in the neuro-surgery theatre and through frequent association with another Victoria giant in Kilmarnock. Norman Davidson, also a consultant in the Victoria, was honorary visiting surgeon to Kilmarnock Infirmary and I now appreciate how fortunate I was to have been trained by such men.

Surgeons accepted risks, some of which were beyond their own control. Anaesthesia was still a vaguely understood mystery carrying risk of sinister post-operative complications; and in these days pneumonia could often be fatal. Risk was reduced by speed and deft surgical technique. Indeed, I remember Lord Bob preaching that a 'major operation was anything which lasted more than one hour'.

The physiology of body fluid loss was only dimly understood and blood transfusions were complicated affairs: partly because there was still a total shortage of donors, but above all, sepsis was the ultimate bug-bear. Wound sepsis could come from an imperfectly sterilised operating theatre; from contaminated pre-packaged material such as cat-gut; from sneezes, coughs or colds; and from bugs spluttered through the operating area from nurses, doctors, or casual visitors. There were no antibiotics, which meant that post-operative pneumonia and all wound sepsis had to be controlled by Nature alone: plus, of course, 'routine nursing measures', as they were called, and which had nothing to do with cure as such. An infected wound might dribble pus for weeks or months.

For men like Norman Davidson or John Peden, Lord Bob, wee Pat or Jim Galloway wound sepsis was the ultimate sin, implying, as it did, a major break-down of aseptic technique, and they reduced risk by every means possible. Theatre sterilisation was a time-consuming and rigorous pre-operative procedure. Any staff member with a suspect throat or head cold was banished until cured. Spot-check smears were taken from swabs, sheets and instruments after preparation to confirm that sterilisation procedures had been effective. Theatre staff 'scrubbed up' for twenty minutes before putting on gloves and any case of wound sepsis which did develop was investigated in detail. Specimens of pus isolated the offending germ, and efforts were made to trace similar germs of the same strain from all persons who had attended during that operation. Everything was geared to abolish sepsis, and, since trauma during an operation favours growth of bacteria upon bruised tissue, these older-day surgeons operated with a soft touch dexterity which has, nowadays, almost been forgotten.

Today even mental attitudes are different. The physiology of fluid loss is now understood and body fluid-chemical balance maintained at all stages during every major operation. Blood transfusions are simple to carry out. Antibiotics 'cure' most cases of chest complications, and even control (note the word 'control') wound infection. Surgeons no longer need to fear sepsis and too many have become technically careless. The fact that results in terms of *life* may be satisfactory has little to do with this particular argument, which suggests that as craftsmen they have far to go before they can be compared with vintage men of pre-war years. During my later years as family doctor, patient after patient was sent home from all sorts of hospitals with pus still leaking from his wounds. It did not seem to matter to many surgeons concerned and there was no apparent sense of shame. It was almost, eventually, even *expected* by many patients who had previous experience of the modern attitude.

In the older days a minor stitch abscess was enough to make a surgeon wish to curl up and hide until the thing had settled down. But today? Who cares? Wonder drugs have given many indifferent surgeons a public halo.

Nor was there any great difference in Scotland between provincial hospitals and teaching units during the pre-World War Two years. Matters, however, were different in England where many provincial hospitals gave extraordinary scope to people who were virtually untrained. Sir Hector MacLennan once told me that he was allowed 'to hold a retractor' only after he had been 'qualified for five years'. If, at the same stage, he had taken a post as resident obstetrician or resident surgical officer in England, he might well have been doing Caesarean sections . . . as I did myself, within three years of qualifying. I also had friends who were coping with appendectomies, any-ectomies, and doing a near-total spectrum of emergency surgery within a month or two of graduation, but only within provincial English hospitals and certain English local authority hospitals. This was never tolerated in pre-war Scotland, where, I would go so far as to claim, a down-and-out taken off the streets with a surgical emergency would have fared much better, and with much higher odds in favour of a cure, than a medium-income house-owning, mid-echelon professional man, who was unable to pay for private facilities in England, and this applied right through from the Channel to the Cheviots.

The English scene has changed. Yet even in England, and in spite of the change, most modern surgeons are still indifferent craftsmen by comparison with the titans of yesterday, and sadly the new student body has few with whom it can make comparisons. My own generation was, and is, one of the last which can remember the qualities required from a surgeon in pre-antibiotic, pre-anything-you-like days.

I recall watching Sir Henry Wade remove a damaged kidney in Edinburgh Royal Infirmary. I was sitting with a few Australian and American surgeons in the gallery while the old man arranged his instruments, and an American turned to me as Sir Henry lifted his scalpel. 'Say, what do you call that old guy?'

He glanced back towards the operating table. 'Jesus Christ' he gasped. Sir Henry was already holding the kidney in his hands, only six or seven seconds later.

The old man looked round mischievously. 'Wrong, sir. Not J.C. The name's Henry Wade.'

And Henry was also one of the great.

My flow of work was interrupted at the Victoria when I found that I was allowed to take a little leave, but I wondered where to go and finally decided to leave everything to Fate. On the day before I was due to start I met a nurse with whom I had been at school. 'Okay. I'm Fate, right?' she said. 'But I've got an aunt in Rotterdam and she has three daughters. I'll wire and ask them to meet you at the morning boat train the day after tomorrow.' Beyond feeling that one never went wrong if one simply left things to Fortune, I agreed, booked for Rotterdam via London and Harwich, got myself organised and stepped off the train wearing the kilt. Kathleen had insisted on this, since, as she explained, it would be easier for her aunt to 'pick me out'.

The aunt turned out to be a bustling little lady of devastating charm. She was too well-mannered to say much about the kilt, but I discovered later that she wondered how her husband would react. Mr Cornelis van der Poest Clement was, and still is, a man who does not care too much for people who seem to be either obtrusive or non-conformist. Her home was along the side of an island on the River Maas, and her second daughter, Trudie, was coming down the stairs when we entered. I knew, in that first second, that we would marry. I had no doubts at all, and felt suddenly 'secure'. It was a wonderfully exhilarating experience simply to know, way-deep-down, that this was already 'decided'.

> She came like a sunbeam dusting the dawn,
> lips inviting love.
> She paused, like a wild thing, shy as a fawn,
> smiling, far above
> a boy like me.
>
> Her voice, like an echo kissing a hill
> came from afar.
> Her words, like a silence, gentle and still
> quietly raised a bar
> and made me free.
>
> Time leapt back on that summer's day
> as lovers, long ago,
> sensed inward, urging voices, say
> 'Once more you meet! You know
> My Way. Just be.
>
> 'I juggled your footsteps and brought you here
> In time of need.
> Your maiden will teach you the conquest of fear
> and raise your seed.
> MY life YOUR tree.'
>
> My living began when I saw Trudie smile.
> Smiles exciting strength,
> banishing fear and cynical guile
> for life's long length.
> To be beloved, her only fee.

That evening Trudie was my partner, with her parents as chaperone, at a dinner dance in Pschorr's, a place-of-happy-memory destroyed during the bombing of Rotterdam in May 1940. The dance floor had panels of coloured glass lit by interior lights and the whole set-up was romantic. Mrs van der Poest Clement also laughed at my teetotal ideas and introduced me to Dutch gin, though her husband was preoccupied and I eventually discovered that he was bothered because I had not completely cleared my plate during dinner, and because my kilt was 'conspicuous'.

We bedded down around two o'clock, and I was still trying to sleep three hours later. It seemed sensible to rise and shave, get downstairs and enjoy the early morning river traffic. Trudie joined me a few moments later and said that she, too, had failed to sleep, so we went for a short walk to the tip of the island, looking down-stream, and after a few moments became unofficially engaged. When I returned some months later to make a sentimental visit to the same spot I found that we had taken the plunge just outside a public convenience.

I also managed by stratagem, to linger for three full days and then took off on a Rhine ship for Germany where young blond gods were all lording it over pliant goddesses. Cologne, however, got me down and the cathedral failed to impress, probably because a number of SS men were goosestepping around the inside, or at least were goosestepping every time they moved. An Australian, with whom I struck up casual contact, then became involved with a girl who turned out to be mistress of a local Party member and we opted to leave Cologne at speed, pausing only at Brüng's Wine Garden to sing *Ein Mal Zum Rhein* and lower a few steins. The Australian then became drunk and eventually picked a quarrel with a man in uniform at Cologne station. When I last saw him he was running at top speed towards the horizon. Meanwhile, and since I had been identified with him, two thin-lipped men with pince-nez and uniform took my own luggage apart, advised me to be more 'respectful towards my host country in future' and left me to make of it what I could.

After eight days at Boppard mixing with Strength Through Joy addicts, I returned to Rotterdam convinced that 'next time' the Germans would keep to the letter of the Schlieffen Plan and invade Holland together with Belgium and France. The only question was 'when'. But I had a new objective in life, to get Trudie out of continental Europe before the first bomb went off.

Trudie was quiet, shy, quadri-lingual and newly returned from school in Lausanne. She disliked 'doctors' because of experiences in early life and was baffled to understand how she could have fallen in love with one. My meeting with her was the most fortunate experience in all life. A few people have recently said: 'I've known Trudie for twenty years (or whatever), but I don't understand her any more than when we first met.' Why should they? And who cares? Trudie believes in sharing her secret thoughts with very few people indeed. She is a creature of nature, beloved by animals and birds alike. She speaks with her flowers and they grow to please her. She is more at ease with quiet brown people on the hills of New Guinea or the more remote Pacific islands than with tycoons in a drawing-room. She can be understood only by those who feel for simple things. A baby robin in our garden will please her more than a panda behind bars. Alpine glow will thrill her more than The Changing of the Guard. A dolphin beside our ship will satisfy her more than the Captain's Cocktail Party. She will find pleasure through wearing a cotton frock, but none from using rabbit or mink. She believes that power corrupts and that 'status' is bad for the soul. She has won the love of our two boys. She has even won the love of their wives. Those who know her best think of her as a 'lady'. Her word is her bond, and as my old teacher Sandy Clark recently said 'she is straight as a die'. She has borne with me patiently, but when my parents heard that Trudie had said 'yes' they looked at me, surprised. 'Summer her and winter her, George,' snapped my mother. 'Time enough to think about marriage then.'

My father was more to the point. 'Is there any insanity in the family?' he asked. Back at the Victoria I said nothing to anyone, secret treasures are better hidden.

From September 1937 onwards life became a simple mixture of routine hospital work, stolen short trips to Rotterdam and the writing of endless letters. But return to hospital was complicated by need to make a surprising decision. My chief, Robert

Tennent, was treating an autocratic private patient from Cape Town who ruled her roost with a rod of iron. Nurses quailed before her, and even sister counted ten before speaking. Bob handled her in his jovially gruff reassuring manner but left me to 'get on with it' and crisis broke when one of my favourite nurses fled from the woman's room in tears. I double-checked what had been going on and decided that a nuisance would have to be abated. The woman was a tyrant.

She was in magnificent form when I arrived to do battle and fired a broadside by damning most of the nursing staff on a score of counts, adding that the food was not fit for a nigger to eat, and rounding off with a few well chosen words about inefficiency in the X-ray department, where, I gathered, she had been kept waiting for a few moments earlier in the morning.

I took over when she paused to breathe and gave an uncensored opinion covering her manners, her attitudes, her bullying and her personality. I spoke from the heart and reminded her that only a most inferior person would aggress against junior nursing staff who were unable to defend themselves. I remember saying that she was the worst type of colonial, and the type who would ultimately bring down the British Empire (prophetic words indeed). The curious thing is that she heard me out without interruption, but when I had covered the situation in detail I was only asked if I would be so good as to leave her room.

She made no comment during any of my routine visits for four or five days, and since my chief said nothing I figured that I was well out of possible trouble. Eventually, however, she requested a mid-evening visit and I went to her room, expecting disaster. I still remember her opening words, 'Sit down, young man, and this time let me do the talking.'

She explained that she was a childless widow and literally a millionairess, produced documents to prove her assets and, even more surprising, a paper showing her association with a hospital in Johannesburg. She claimed to have sufficient authority within that hospital to guarantee my appointment to the surgical staff and swift promotion to full charge of my own unit within a few years. She would found it herself if necessary! Her social prestige was such that she also guaranteed me 'a hefty cut of all private practice in the area', and asked only one thing in return.

All that would be mine, and in addition she would make me her sole heir, given that I legally foreswore my family, became her adopted son and accepted her name. Looking back, I find it odd that I turned down offer of marriage to a girl plus £60,000, an offer of a new mother plus a £1,000,000 in the same year, if not in the same six months, and I still wonder why I never gave her offer any real consideration. Documents were by her bedside awaiting study and solicitors in a nearby ante-room. There was no possibility of my losing out on the money.

She was also quite elderly and a poor life risk so it was reasonable to believe that I would be a millionaire before I was thirty-five, yet I did not even think about it seriously. However, it was a moment of truth and proved that I was more deeply attached to my parents and family than I had realised. Surely it is true to say that I was able to prove that I loved my family more than I loved a million sterling? Which is a solemn thought!

Near the end of my Victoria term a chief reminded me that there is no better training ground for a general surgeon than a stint in general practice, and that if I took a job in the district I would still be able to continue my research work in the Victoria laboratories. The idea made sense. Hinton Robertson, another much respected Victoria surgeon, had 'specialised' only after years of family doctoring, and his particular skill in clinical diagnosis was reputed to have come, in part at least, from G.P. There was no impression, during these years, that family doctors were inferior persons who had failed to make the grade as specialists. They were rated as men of quality and there was tremendous mutual loyalty. Today matters are rather different. Few 'specialists' on the hospital side have any real experience of what it means to assume total responsibility, or of what is involved, in terms of challenge, for family doctors, and there is now, in many areas, little or no mutual loyalty.

For many years the general practitioner had reason to feel that the State discriminated against him in terms of both salary and status by comparison with hospital colleagues and this also generated hostility. Too often hospital staff have been unsympathetic to family doctors' problems and further increased that hostility. Hospital grades are still reluctant to admit that family doctors are specialists in their own right within a field which requires not only sound knowledge and experience but the courage of 'loners' who are willing to stand on their own feet. Man for man, I would say that until the later '60s the general practitioner was a superior animal in terms of character. He met the world with its problems while hospital staff sheltered behind white coats, nurses, 'regulations' and the implied authority of any building where they served. Today the family doctor tends, all too often, to do the same thing by sheltering behind protective gambits evolved from the Appointments System, Health Centres and systems of roster duty and so is demoting himself in status while he continues to lose respect annually. It is all very sad. It is even more unfortunate that new generations of teachers are doing little to raise ethical standards, since so many, themselves, are pygmies by comparison with the *average* of the pre-N.H.S. and pre-antibiotic era.

My own baptisms of fire were received in tough areas, and during most of 1938 I was 'part-time assistant' to family doctors in either Paisley or Barrhead. My salary worked out at around £125 per annum, out of which I had to pay my own travelling expenses, and my chiefs estimated 'part-time' as meaning something around eight to ten hours work per day. Broadly speaking, I did top floor visits, most of the 'surgery' work, sessions with chronic sick or the aged, and every awkward person on the list who could be off-loaded by exasperated seniors. I began, in fact, to cut my teeth and learn what it was all about.

General practice separates men from the boys.

6 GENERAL PRACTICE SEPARATES MEN FROM THE BOYS

Doctor Grier of Barrhead was suave, portly and a bachelor whose life was organised by two sisters, Aggie and Bella, who made an impression upon Trudie when they first met by saying: 'Oh! You're the one that's caught him, have ye? Well, ye'll never be as much use as a sister. Every time Jimmy's out at night I get up to see him off, and when he comes back there's always a cup of tea ready. Which is more than a wife will do.'

Bella was a tough baby.

Aggie was small, gristly and domineering.

Between them Dr James Grier toed the sisterly line and caused no domestic trouble.

He had a small flock of pet private patients in Kilmacolm, a snob district then (and a snob district now) but since pet private patients meant a little money from time to time each had an invisible label: 'Fragile. Treat with Extreme Care.'

My first visit to the most petted private patient of all ended in catastrophe. The man was a truculent city tycoon who had sprained his ankle by tripping upon a carpet. Or so he said. More probably he had slipped while drunk. Be that as it may, he had a sprained ankle, and I decided to apply an adhesive elastoplast bandage.

I can still see him glaring at it as he growled: 'What's that?'

'A bandage.'

'Ah can see that, you damn't fool. What kind of bandage?'

'An Elastoplast adhesive bandage.'

'Well take it away. I'm allergic to Elastoplast. Come out all over in spots.'

The word 'allergic' was new to me. After five years at medical school and one in hospital I had not even heard of allergy, so I decided to bluff. Allergy, whatever it was, could not be important! 'Forget it, sir. The new bandages have got something in them to fix that.'

He looked at me suspiciously. 'That so?'

'A recent development,' I said. I lifted his ankle as I spoke and began to wrap the bandage on, beginning at his toes as instructed by my teachers. He was still doubtful, but he let me get on with it and, after I had finished, rang for a maid-servant to show me out. 'Remind God in your prayers to make sure that that new thing works' he said as I left the room.

I forgot about him until late evening when our phone rang and I watched Dr Grier's face which turned crimson as he got the gist of a message. Even I could understand what was being said from the other side of the room. The Kilmacolm sprained ankle was 'out all over' in the daddy of all rashes. My principal looked at me without mercy and his eyes were very cold. 'Get into the car. We're in this together, but answer me, are you insured with the medical protection people?' The question was a sensible one.

The lady of the house was on the steps to greet us. 'So *this* is the young man,' she said venomously – and flounced into the crimson darkness of a vast entrance hall. Even the two maid-servants sniffed as we passed them, one on either side of the first stair, while upstairs the patient's remarks were unprintable even by 1973 standards. I remember only his peroration. 'You miserable child, you. Heavens! What devil possessed you, Grier, to take on a stupid bastard who hasn't got out of nappies yet?'

I decided to go down fighting, and threatened to sue him for calling me a bastard. I said that he had called me stupid in front of witnesses and added that he could not touch or criticise me so long as I had given of my best. He could prove no neglect. My defence triggered off a new stream of abuse. Hadn't he told me that he was allergic to Elastoplast? Stout denial was my only defence . . . so I stoutly denied and asked where were his witnesses.

The question annoyed him, but when he tried to get out of bed he again hurt his ankle, and his screams could have been heard in Bridge of Weir. 'You're a bully,' I remember saying. 'And I don't like bullies. Now turn over and we'll get the bandage off. Though the chances are you ate something.' He became even more crimson: of course he had eaten something, did I expect him to starve?

I had also neglected to shave his leg, and when I ripped the bandage off he was ripe for murder. 'Fire him, Grier,' he yelped, waggling a finger which quivered with fury. 'Fire him or I get another doctor.'

This was the first time I heard a patient issue the penultimate threat – (the ultimate threat is to threaten legal proceedings or complain to the Medical Practices Committee, but the change of doctor approach is much more common. Indeed I soon came to rate it as old hat). Even so, it came as chilly news when heard for the first time. 'Sorry, Doctor Grier,' I said. 'But accept my resignation. And I'll forget any salary due.'

I was leaving the room while Grier was still trying to find words when the patient barked an order. 'Hi! You! Come back here you whippersnapper.'

It was the beginning of a friendship which lasted until he died six months or more later. I gathered that he approved of people who could stand up for themselves, and that when I offered to forgo outstanding salary he could not believe his ears. He seems to have drastically reappraised the situation and decided to give me another chance. But he taught me several lessons. Don't knuckle down to threats, and if a patient gives advice listen to it and follow it. Also check that insurance cover is always paid by banker's draft!

I was nearly broke by the end of my first week and Dr Grier made no mention of salary. At the end of the second week I was flat broke, and there was still no mention. Half way through the third week I had begun to borrow money and decided to ask my principal for my earnings. He seemed surprised and enquired how much he owed. The question took me off-guard and I became flustered. The financial side had not been gone into with any depth when I accepted the job, but I had figured on something around five pounds per week.

'How much?' he asked again.

I became even more confused. The man was a friend of my mother's unmarried sister, Gretta, and I did not want to put a foot wrong. 'I don't know.'

He opened a wallet and counted out a few notes. 'Will ten do?'

I thought he was talking about ten *per week*. 'That's too much.'

73

He whipped off one fiver and handed it across. 'Okay. Two ten per week. Five for a fortnight. You'll be due the next two and a half on Friday.'

The incident taught me to be business-like and never ashamed to talk money. And never, just never, to refuse it when offered!

The practice ran on quite straightforward 'conning' lines. We did our own dispensing and had a cough bottle to help people 'get their spit up'. We had a cough bottle to help people 'compose their cough'. We also had an enormous bottle of white emulsion which covered most digestive upsets, and several Winchesters full of a mixture which was said to be a tonic. The 'poison cupboard' was locked and since James Grier kept the key, I didn't need to worry about morphia even when I felt that it might have been a good idea. We also had a bucketful of ointment to remove spots, another to soothe spots, and still another to 'bring spots to a head'. Nor can I forget the shampoos for lice, which were common as the flowers in spring.

Surgeries were busy, house calls non-stop and the episode unrewarding. My laboratory activities in the Victoria suffered and commonsense told me that it was time to go elsewhere. James Grier had the grace of a high-court judge and the style of an archbishop. His bedside manner was reassuring while his gentle smile and faintly apologetic facial signals seemed to spell out the wisdom of the ages, but behind it there was nothing. I found it all rather sad, and moved on to a no-nonsense practice in Paisley where the principal, Dr Dale, was also a bachelor. Dale was smallish and plump, seldom seen without a bowler hat, and strictly commercial. As part-time assistant to a two-man partnership I speedily found my level. The darker closes, higher tenement flats, more impoverished patients and most of the routine 'surgery' work became my very own world and most patients took a guarded view of 'the new helper'.

Life, in fact, was grim until New Year's Eve, 1938 when I managed to wangle a couple of hours off duty to skate at a Glasgow ice-rink. My effort to do a figure eight backwards ended with one almighty purler on the ice and the swift development of a black eye. I was due to start work at an evening 'surgery' shortly afterwards, and when I walked through the waiting-room conversation stopped. My eye won instantaneous audience attention and I heard a voice say with reluctant admiration: 'Jesus! No' six o'clock yet, and the helper's been at the bottle already. Did ye ever see a better shiner?' I was accepted from that moment on and the Paisley ball was at my feet.

My next surgery began with a sixteen-year-old whose eyes were glowing with admiration. 'They tell me you fair beat the place up on Hogmanay. Imagine! An' they a' thought you were mealy-mouthed.' She was undressing as she spoke and did a complete strip in record time. 'What do you think?' she asked. I remember the conversation to this day. 'About these.' She was stark naked and pointing to her breasts. 'They say ma tits is too wee. Can ye do something about?'

I felt myself blushing.

'Hot in here,' she continued. 'Though ma mither says it's seasonable for the time of year. But come on. Do something. I didnae come here tae waste yur time.'

'They look nice to me,' I said.

'But ah want an examination. Feel them. You know. A friend says they're kinda tight. Is they all right?'

I went through the motions of palpating her breasts and noticed that she was suddenly breathing quickly, getting pale round the lips and wriggling her thighs. 'Feeling okay?' I asked.

She grimaced slightly and closed her eyes. 'Go on, doctor. Squeeze them hard.' She began to gasp, and that was that. 1938 began with my first patient having an orgasm in my surgery, apparently because rumour had put me into the he-man class.

She relaxed for a few seconds while I tried to figure how one got out of this sort of mess, and then she quietly reached for her clothes. 'Do the same for you some time, doctor, and I'll be in to see you next week.' She pulled out a cigarette. 'Here's a fag.'

I figured it was better to co-operate. She lit it with fingers which were still slightly shaky and inhaled deeply. 'Ah always feel great after a wee bit fun, doctor.' I forget the rest of her lines, but she stubbed out her cigarette in the sink and was about to leave when she put her hand to her mouth. 'Ah nearly forgot, but they sent me tae get Faither's bottle. The red yin. Mither says the green yin sent him to the closet.'

So I learned yet another lesson. When I was running my own

practice I never allowed any girl to undress without a nurse being present or a secretary standing by a slightly open door, and any girl who looked emotionally complicated was never seen alone under any circumstances. But secretaries and nurses were unheard of luxuries in the pre-war Dale-Black practice and I suppose we all ran theoretical risks daily.

The year also began with an unfortunate incident involving one of the Dale private patients. A so-called emergency call was on the telephone pad when I returned one morning for coffee and I took it almost automatically. The house was pretentious and set back from the road among quite imposing gardens, while the house-maid, who answered my bell-signal, looked at me curiously, sniffed and said briefly. 'You're no' Doctor Dale.'

I ignored her and walked into the usual large hall where a house-keeper type in black looked at me even more curiously. 'You're no' Doctor Dale.' I explained that I was the assistant and would be glad if she took me to the patient's bedroom. I realised that I had snapped into a sort of parade-ground voice, but thought nothing of it until we met a man coming down the stairs whose voice boomed out from above as he stopped in his tracks. 'YOU'RE NO' DOCTOR DALE.'

I explained that I was the assistant, but was interrupted. 'Helper, man. Helper. Speak the language.' His voice rose by a few hundred decibels. 'Wife. You upstairs. Dale's sent the helper.'

I gritted my teeth and made for an open door in the landing above. Nor was I surprised when a smallish woman with a thin nose and wire-framed spectacles looked at me curiously, saying with a disgusted sniff. 'You're not Doctor Dale.'

After explanations I discovered that she had a severe headache and decided to leave some codeine tablets from my bag. She looked at them suspiciously. 'If that's aspirin I'll have you know that aspirin disagrees with me.' I assured her ten times over that not only were they not aspirin, but that they did not contain any aspirin and would do her no harm. I even waited until she had swallowed two before leaving the house. It was an hour later, and while confining a young mother with her first child, that I remembered how I had run out of codeine tablets and filled the bottle labelled codeine with APC tablets, and that

APC meant aspirin, phenacetin and codeine (or maybe caffeine. But some other 'eine'). I also remembered that Doctor Dale was a different proposition from James Grier of Barrhead, and that I was likely to be fired without a testimonial when he heard about it. If, indeed, the wretched woman really was allergic to aspirin. That she was I discovered at lunch-time when Dale arrived to blast me to smithereens. The woman had 'come out all over' with nettle rash.

Only one thing saved me. He was curious to know how I had managed to get near the bed at all, since no one in the house would have anything to do with any doctor other than himself. The fact that they had 'seen' me somehow put me on the same level as himself and the situation intrigued him. Conversation became more civilised and ended with the little man clamping his bowler firmly down over the eyes and remarking to the air around that 'he was buggered if he could understand, but any helper who got through to that lot must have something in him'.

So the world marched on while I skated on the thinnest of ice, making mistake after mistake, but, so far as I know, killing no one either through mis-diagnosis or neglect. I had a considerable following of teen-age female fans, since the black-eye incident was not quickly forgotten, and several were cunning in their efforts. Several night-calls took me to flats where wooden floors were covered only with a scrap of rug, and the built-in bed was almost glamorous under candle-light or a pink bedside electric bulb. The alleged patient was always alone, looking as seductive as it was possible for a slum girl with no money to be, and clearly ready for anything. Excuse for the calls was usually flimsy: a 'sore belly' or a 'terrible pain down below' or a 'stabbing pain in the heart doctor' or 'ah'm feart because mah heart's going too fast'. Once, and once only, an eighteen-year-old blonde threw back the bed-clothes and smiled from ear to ear. 'Betty said ye give good massage. Ah could do wi' some.'

The interesting thing, looking back, was the 'innocence' of these girls. I don't believe they were dangerous, they were just out for traditional kicks, and the black-eye affair made them rate me as one of their own caste. Fortunately, being 'part-time' I had few nights on duty, other than to 'oblige' a principal when on leave, but when I was on call almost anything could happen.

Wife-beating situations, head stitchings, battered baby problems, the occasional attempted suicide and frightened old people living alone became my familiars, but one problem at least has now been removed by the Welfare State. I had become accustomed to undernourished infants lying in a corner of every ward in hospital. Now, fortunately, it is almost impossible to see a 'marasmic baby', though as assistant in general practice I saw one or more every week. During fifteen years in general practice after the National Health Service began I never saw even one. Infants which have become familiar to all the world through television coverage of famine in Asia were almost commonplace in pre-World-War-Two Britain, but how many of our latter day malcontents who continually scream for more, and more, and more of the nation's cake realise what a very large cut they have already been given? Also, if progress has not been sufficiently fast for a few professional mud-stirrers who now want everything done 'yesterday', how many of them are ever heard to praise achievements which are already truly great? It is also interesting that throughout my pre-war year in general practice I recall no real class bitterness or any class hatred. But now, even after tremendous strides forward, and a standard of living having been reached which could never even have been imagined or dreamed of by the Hunger Marchers I remember as a child, now, even with no poor-houses, no risk of starvation, free medicare and no significant caste gulf whatever, there is real class hatred and bitterness built upon ignorance and greed.

Many other diseases have also gone. Where is rickets in 1974 or the 'bandy-legged' children of even 1938? Where is tuberculosis or killing diphtheria? Where are the young with chronically swollen neck glands? Where are young chronic bronchitics? And where are the pale, chronically-anaemic or semi-undernourished children? Rising youngsters must be among the most healthy in the world, yet how many parents or grandparents pause to consider the miracles which have been worked through only two or three decades? Too many take everything for granted, and rampant greed became the national curse starting as far back as the later fifties. The near revolutionary situation of 1972–74 was predictable by any person in the confidence of many 'workers' years before it actually developed.

On the medical side it is interesting now to compare what family doctors accepted as normal routine in the old days with what they are prepared to do in 1974. Minor operations, the opening of boils, snicking of abscesses, repair of even fairly extensive wounds, forceps deliveries in slum houses, stretchings of fore-skins, coping with minor fractures and controlling post-dental haemorrhages or nose bleeds were taken in their stride. Complicated splints for arm or leg fractures were applied almost as a first-aid adjunct to treatment, but, when they *did* request admission of a patient to hospital it was seldom refused. Indeed, in the old days, it was almost more than a house officer's final testimonial was worth to refuse a hospital admission.

On the hospital side resident doctors accepted that any 're-ceiving' night might end with a double row of emergency beds down the centre of the ward and left it to their chiefs to reduce over-crowding in the morning. By the middle fifties, and within my own experience, it often became difficult even to get semi-emergencies admitted to most hospitals within my area. Junior house-doctors would, without hesitation, refuse admission of quite seriously ill people, and if I attempted to deal direct with more senior people below consultant level there was often argument or shilly-shallying. This, of course, reflected the impaired relationship which existed between hospital staff and G.P.s. But it was unheard of in earlier days.

And in the same way, appointment systems in hospital out-patient departments have now become ridiculous. In the 'old days' it was enough to send a patient up to the first available out-patient clinic covering his requirements, and that was seldom more than one day ahead. He was always 'seen' and his problem laid on the conveyor belt through all necessary investigations. Now, with the appointment system, delay of weeks is common, and this is clearly impossible.

The appointments system is even more unsatisfactory in general practice, and I resisted it to the bitter end. But then I had learned my basic training the hard way, and in 'the old days' a surgery session could, and did, last for four or five hours. I frequently started a session in Paisley at around four o'clock and quit only around nine, by which time one of the principals had taken over. It follows that a patient had no need to 'wait' for more than two or three hours. Years later, when I was running my own practice, every patient was seen when requested and none waited for more than upwards of two hours (chiefly because I had a smaller 'list' than the Dale-Black show of 1938). Within a few months of the appointment system being introduced consultations were delayed for upwards of a week, which is both inefficient and dangerous. So in that respect the 'old days' were better. But by 'old days' in this sense, I mean days right up to the introduction of that clinically impracticable nonsense of an appointments system.

From most other points of view patients have never been so fortunate. The pre-antibiotic era required of the family doctor a capacity for diagnosis which would enable him to single out people with significant illness from those who were complaining of trivia. A proportion were then off-loaded to hospital, but the family doctor still accepted responsibility for serving coronaries, pneumonias, terminal malignancies, the chronic sick and innumerable other everyday problems. Since he could do nothing but relieve symptoms, and since his battery of even pain-relieving drugs was both small and relatively ineffective, he had to rely upon sheer force of personality, bluff, a reassuring bedside manner and a close doctor-patient relationship to achieve success. Few patients threatened to 'change' their doctor, few doctors 'poached' upon a colleague's preserves, and there was stability. But there it ended. Treatment was sophisticated witchdoctoring.

Patients did accept that many would die, but nowadays wonder drugs are taken for granted and the eternal cry is 'something must be done'. It is unfortunate that only a very, very few ever pause to think of what has already been done. Blood transfusion is now as much part of living as the package tour to Spain. Quality antenatal care is part of the ordinary scene, like a family car and television. Life-saving immunisations are often accepted only with a grudge by uptight young parents afraid that the 'needle may hurt', otherwise they are commonplace as the record player, the radio and the fridge. So the list could be extended indefinitely, but the tragedy is that people still demand more, and more and more. Indeed, acute infections are now supposed to get better 'yesterday'.

One other fascinating mystery is the attitude of men towards their wives. In 'the old days' before 1947 men did not want to be off work for one 'shift' longer than was absolutely essential and women had to be half dying on their feet before they would 'give in and see the doctor'. Non-white-collar workers have now achieved standards of material comfort unimagined in 1938, but when a man does lie up on Monday with, for example, a minor sickness which should be clear in a couple of days he will seldom go back to work in less than a week. A man who takes ill on, say, a Friday, will seldom return before one week on the following Monday. The three day licence to be off work without a doctor's certificate has also cost the country millions of working hours, as Mr Kenneth Robinson himself admitted to me when he was shadow Minister of Health. Yet this licence is still abused by thousands of men *most of whom would not allow their wives to rest for one whole day if they were suffering from the same condition*. No trade-union in Britain would tolerate the working conditions which many of these men have imposed upon their wives. A woman must now be *really* ill before all-too-many husbands will tolerate her spending a few days in bed. Wives with, say, influenza-type illnesses are fortunate if they manage two or three days off work, whereas their men will seldom settle for less than ten. The Welfare State has not only encouraged laziness; it has made laziness profitable.

Not so in other years. During my first sessions in general practice I found few who complained of working conditions. There was, to repeat, virtually no class hatred or bitterness whereas now there is, and this fact was confirmed by Lord Shinwell during a 'World at One' programme in 1971. People used to say of a person who was seeking the impossible that he was 'reaching for the moon'. It seems that since the moon has now been reached an enormous number of work-shy layabouts believe that the impossible can really happen, and that they can continue to live, for free, from cradle to the grave, plus of course, car and holidays.

In spite of their poverty, many of the people I worked among were happier then than they are today, and I found, within the slums, a good fellowship and courage which was inspiring. This was one of the happiest professional years of my life. I felt 'wanted' by my flock of petty mobsters, amateur prostitutes, card-sharps, political agitators, bookies' runners, drunks, pimps and jail-birds, widows, pensioners, and simple folk. My black-eye had given me a free pass to their society and I felt privileged. Months after I had left Paisley I met Doctor Dale at a motor show and I cherish his words. 'I didn't realise you were so popular till you had gone. A lot of them have been wanting to know why we didn't make you a partner.'

My last surgery was a sad break. Rumour had got around that I was leaving and the waiting-room was packed. Scots are in-articulate and compliments come only with difficulty, but all managed to say something to make me feel good and vanity has made me remember two asides which were short and to the point. There was the docker who shook my hand and said, 'Staun' ye a pint ony night doc. Ye ken the pub.' And Betty, the girl who had introduced my Paisley New Year! 'Ye ken the hoose, doctor. Ah keep masel' clean an' ye can get a good time. Yer wee lassie'll never know.'

When it was all over I went back to the Victoria and began to wind up my experiments. They had continued for nearly eighteen months and I figured that I had worked out a laboratory test to diagnose early cases of thyrotoxicosis. It remained only to write my thesis and sit the clinical examination.

The end-point was graduation as Doctor of Medicine in April, 1939 and Trudie came over for the show. I wore a mortar-board and gown together with my M.B., Ch.B. hood and felt more self-conscious than I had done wearing the kilt at Pschorr's. I reckoned that the small success had depended chiefly upon luck and felt more phoney than ever. Even so, I hoped that I would be equally lucky in Edinburgh. The Royal College of Surgeons is a distinguished 'club' and I was not optimistic. But I had no options. The ambitions of my parents seemed to be insatiable and when they heard that I had satisfied the M.D. examiners my father's only comment had been brief. 'See and pass the Fellowship. It's worth more than an M.D.' Nor could I forget that when I passed the 'final' examinations in medicine his only comment had then been equally brief. 'What will you take next?' I sometimes wondered if either of them ever knew how much I wanted to hear just one simple word of praise.

Their attitudes worried several people and it was at this stage that Craig Borland began his campaign to have my brother Alistair sent to boarding school, this being, in his view, the only reasonable escape from influences which could eventually cripple him emotionally as an adult.

Nor had Trudie been given an easy passage. She was accepted but we were chaperoned as though living at the turn of the century. If we returned home in the late evening detailed explanations as to how we had passed our time and where we had been became unavoidable, and the family found no absurdity in treating their 'doctor' son as an immature and irresponsible schoolboy. It was many years before they began, perhaps, to realise how fortunate they had been in meeting Trudie and to understand how she always chose to try and find reasons for their behaviour, to look below the surface and to find excuses for their fears. The fact that she began eventually to love them did more than anything to improve my own relationship with parents whom I still feared.

7 SURGERY FOR BEGINNERS

I graduated M.B., Ch.B. at 22 and M.D. at 24. A college regulation, however, prohibited Fellowship until the candidate was 25, but certain sub-chiefs held tutorial classes for the examinations, and I enrolled under John Bruce, later Sir John Bruce, Professor of Surgery and President of the College.

Sir John is the finest teacher I ever met. Lucid, painstaking and explicit it was a privilege to hear him lecture, while practical attendance at operating sessions within Sir John Fraser's Professorial Unit made the cram course unforgettable.

Examinations were scheduled for March, 1939, but my birthday was in May so I was ineligible by two months. Even so, I decided to run through the routine and discover exactly what was involved. Obviously I did not expect 'to pass'. A week or two later, however, I received official notification that I had 'satisfied the examiners' and the news put me into a flat spin. I was too young by several weeks, yet I was scared to try my luck a second time so in the end I thanked my stars and became a Fellow. But I was unhappy about the age angle and remained unhappy right on until 1967 when, on a day when I was lunching with Sir John, by then President of the College, I decided to confess, though I was, by that time, no longer engaged in active surgery. Even so I felt that I was at risk. The College might – just might – decide to discipline me, but Sir John was only amused and let the matter ride. I still feel that it was a freak pass. Many come, but only a minority percentage is chosen and one part of me still says that I could never have done it again. However, I had become quite well qualified, on paper at least, and had a sound theoretical knowledge of technical essentials.

John Peden's brother-in-law was consultant ear, nose and throat surgeon (oto-rhino-laryngologist) to the Warneford Hospital, Leamington Spa, and a job was arranged through the 'chum club' as Resident Surgical Officer.

Leamington was delightful and the Warneford a snug set-up

with a vaguely 'county' atmosphere. My chief was Gerald Alderson of unforgettable memory. He was handsome, tanned, with unruly black hair streaked with grey, an attractive lay-out of crinkly laughter lines and a vaguely cruel smile. His hobby was horse-riding and he played Sir Simon de Montfort at the Kenilworth Festival, storming up the steps on his charger like a suicidal crusader determined to slaughter an infinite number of Saracens before dying bravely with his lance in one hand and a bible in the other.

My first contact with reality came fourteen hours after arrival when I discovered that the Resident Surgical Officer was expected to cope with a Saturday morning ear, nose and throat session. Two mastoids and six or seven tonsillectomies (with adenoids) were on the list, and the sub-chief on duty insisted that it was my job. He was a G.P. who did part-time hospital work and was astonished by my lack of enthusiasm. He might have been even more astonished had he known that I had never once seen a mastoid opened up, or for that part, been nearer to a tonsil and adenoidectomy than seven or eight feet.

He did the first mastoid himself and then 'handed over'.

Hours later I completed my mutilation of the last throat and three-quarters or more of the two final tonsils lay in a kidney dish. I was soaked in sweat and tense as a bow-string, but I had coped, and added another 'first' to my collection. My conscience, however, was again in rebellion. Would I, I asked myself, have been content if the butchery carried out had been directed against a child of my own?

Worse, sadly, was to follow.

Gerald Alderson was a ladies' man. They adored him, and little wonder, because he was handsome and in all ways manly. There was nothing of the effeminate about Gerald, but never did I imagine that he would, from time to time, invite lady friends up to watch him operate. Or that I would, on such occasions, be his whipping-boy. Yet so it proved.

Five ladies (not women: Gerald socialised only with ladies) had coffee beforehand while I scrubbed up and dealt with preliminaries. Gerald, of course, had joined them, and their merry laughter rang in everyone's ears as we prepared a man for prostatectomy. Gerald then arrived resplendent, having changed into what, as I recall, were grass green pants and sleeveless shirt. A short time later the session began and I was bawled out for failing to snip a stitch correctly. Raps across the knuckles followed from time to time, and I soon gathered that he was determined to underline a point. It was being made clear to the ladies that the operation was difficult, if not actually dangerous, and that Gerald could win through only if everyone was on tip-toe.

Talk about a Roman holiday! The operating suite became a sort of latter day amphitheatre with Gerald playing Emperor while his victims died the death. I was hot with combined indignation and amusement when the session finally closed and the ladies departed. Nor was it much consolation to hear him say as they were leaving: 'that new chap looks quite good'. When he joined me in the side-room he was jovial, relaxed and friendly, I basked in the sunshine of his smile and accepted that it had all been a game. He could have disarmed Satan!

Such was my initiation into surgery in one of England's privileged areas. Within weeks I was doing Caesarean sections, responsible emergency surgery and a quota of 'cold' surgery which made my blood freeze. No man could have felt less competent, and I was always extremely surprised when a patient recovered.

A euthanasia situation unexpectedly loomed up when I discovered a few elderly people with advanced malignancies lying in a row of beds in one particular ward. My work took me into several units, since Gerald, though senior surgeon, was not my only chief. 'What a pity,' said night sister when I was doing a late ward round, 'to think that by this time tomorrow these nice old men will all be in the mortuary.'

Explanations proved that such people were, from time to time, killed by one or other doctor after an operating session. Death certificates were issued without question and there seemed to be no problems with the coroner. The actual mercy killings went according to plan. A genial character joked with the patient for a few seconds while he injected an enormous intra-venous dose of evipan. The patient was asleep within a minute or so and very dead within hours. The whole affair was conducted without fuss and was so 'civilised' that I accepted it without even pausing to think. I knew that 'English law was different from Scots law' and somehow one part of me took it for granted that the euthanasia routine was legal. I even coped with one or two myself, and without any conflict. *It was normal.* Everyone was doing it, so to speak. It was just that I had not been properly educated and had not realised the difference between Scotland and England.

It was, of course, completely illegal and totally unethical, but I still say that it was merciful to the people concerned. It saved them weeks or months of pain, worry and possibly even fear, and I still consider that euthanasia, conducted without making a major production out of it, is the ideal end-point for many types of terminal illness including many conditions other than cancer. We shall hear much more of it during the next twenty years. Eventually it will be accepted by society.

One patient, however, lingers in mind. She was in the middle forties and completely informed about her condition, which was bad. Expectation of life could be measured only in months and she was already having biggish doses of pain-killing drugs several times per day. I spoke with her frequently and an evening came when she asked if I would do her a favour. She explained that her house was now in order, her will organised, and that she had seen her family with friends while she was still looking reasonably well. She had had her hair dressed for the occasion and wished to be remembered by them when looking 'half decent'. There was now nothing left for her to do but die. She wished me to take her into a side room, lay on certain music from a favourite disc, and then, when she gave me the signal, allow her to go out using a suitable injection.

I did exactly as she wished, and she squeezed my hand while listening to the second movement of Beethoven's Ninth Symphony. I then slipped the needle into a large vein and gave her an enormous dose of suitable drugs. She slept swiftly and died in less than an hour. Her last words were whispered, but clear. 'Thank you. Thank you so very, very much.'

Weeks later I did something which left me with intermittent sorrow right to the present day. A girl had been admitted dead within minutes of a road accident. She was at term with her second pregnancy and the foetal heart was still beating so I did a swift section in the out-patient department and delivered a lovely infant.

How could I have known that it would be born blind?

How could I have known that the mother was separated from her husband and that the father was unknown?

How could I have guessed that her parents would refuse to accept the child, and that it was doomed to be brought up in an institution?

After that experience nothing would have again persuaded me to interfere with nature.

It was also during early Leamington days that every doctor in Britain received an official flimsy from Charles (now Lord) Hill, then secretary to the British Medical Association. The flimsy anticipated outbreak of war and requested doctors to tick an appropriate column. Were they prepared to offer service at home, service abroad, or service at home or abroad. I ticked off 'at home or abroad' and returned it immediately.

War broke out some months later and almost caught me on leave in Scandinavia with Trudie and her family. We were in Copenhagen when it became clear that trouble would break, and we flew back to Rotterdam with hours to spare. I paused long enough on the way to Leamington to see Neville Chamberlain being reassuring outside Downing Street, to hear that first abortive air-raid siren which reminded Londoners that they were at war, and to watch sandbags begin to build up around Admiralty Arch.

Leamington was more beautiful than ever. The gardens were ablaze with colour and swans on the Leam swam proudly in line with half-grown cygnets.

I then tried to get Trudie into Britain and still do not understand why she was refused a visa. After many weeks there was a complete *impasse* and I became desperate. That apart, I was expecting to be called up any day, and wondering why Charles Hill's minions did not do something about the flimsy which had now become important. Work load had slumped to near zero and only very real emergencies required attention, so I had time to think.

Outbreak of war caused a sudden national epidemic of good health. Life in the hospital was boring and Gerald decently allowed me more time off to visit Holland and get married, yet that also became more difficult than I had expected, and it was Christmas before permission to leave Britain came through. My train left Victoria Station from platform 13. My reserved seat was number 13. My aircraft seat number was 13, and when I sat down there was a row of 13 suggestive marks forward of my body. This, I was told was due to a German fighter having shot the aeroplane up a week or two earlier. I decided, when we landed safely, that 13 was my lucky number.

Ice was flowing on the Maas and Rotterdam sparkled under diamond-glinting frost. Yet the Dutch authorities refused to marry us because I had no birth certificate with me. Nor could I persuade our local consul to allow Trudie a visa, so I returned to Leamington and contacted Anthony Eden direct. My letter was brief, but he reacted promptly and Trudie arrived in Britain on January 21st. The customs authorities charged her £20 duty on her wedding dress and we reached Leamington prepared to live happily ever after. Gerald Alderson was kind and allowed her to sleep in hospital for a few days while we organised digs. He even allowed me a further week of leave in February and we got married in Glasgow University Chapel on February 21st, 1940 where I turned to watch my bride come up the aisle and knew that I had never seen anything so lovely. She was alone. Her parents were still in Holland, and she was shy. She was surrounded only by strangers, yet she walked, radiant, to my side and she has remained there ever since.

A month or two later a morning broadcast criticised British doctors for having failed to volunteer for service in the Forces, a charge so preposterous, remembering the circular which had been sent out, that I went direct to London and found several hundred other angry doctors protesting in B.M.A. House.

Charles Hill, with his usual play-it-cool technique, allowed the storm to blow itself out and an instruction was finally issued to the meeting by a secretary. 'Would all gentlemen holding "higher qualifications" step into the next room?' I joined the small élite and expected to be made a major on the spot. In point of fact, I was quizzed about lack of 'practical' experience and told that I would be 'called' when required.

With that cold comfort I returned to Leamington determined to eat, love, and be merry. My days in 'civvies' would be numbered. It was time to start making hay while any sun was left to shine, and that particular summer was very lovely. The candles on chestnut trees were enormous and bursting with promise, every swan seemed to have cygnets and the Leam glowed like an Impressionist painting around our punt. The palm court orchestra played our favourite melodies and, since I had come to know the leader, they covered more Lehar and Strauss than usual, yet never forgetting our own very personal song, *Violetta*.

We also rode in Kenilworth woods and I shall never forget the thrill of galloping across acres of bluebells blurring to a carpet of greenish-helio as trot broke into canter and canter into gallop. Stratford, Coventry, Birmingham and the Cotswolds provided everything from dinner-dances and the theatre to hill walks across country still unspoiled, while at the Warneford I began, slowly, to acquire just a little confidence – which was all very well, but I still remember Leamington as a place of shattering surprises and the first clear denial of my Hippocratic Oath. A Hospital Board meeting was held at regular intervals and I was obliged to attend when summoned. The first occasion taught me much. A number of tweedy ladies and hearty gentlemen were grouped around an oval table with my chief on one side and Doctor Berry, the Chairman, presiding. They welcomed me with jovial 'huzzahs' or country-style whoops and immediately got down to brass tacks.

'Tell me, Mr Mair,' said one lady wearing a flat pork-pie hat, and with a fishing hook plus fly in her lapel, 'my man so-and-so is a patient in ward such-and-such. Exactly what is the matter with him?'

I was dumbfounded and glanced towards Gerald Alderson for moral support. My chief, however, seemed preoccupied with the grain of the wood in front of him and refused to catch my eye. 'I'm sorry, ma'am. I'm not allowed to discuss my patients.'

She looked at me curiously. 'Speak up. Speak up. What's wrong with the fellow?'

I refused to give any information and Doctor Berry suggested that I have a word with my chief in private. The 'word' was interesting. The Hospital Board asked questions and I answered them or was fired. They were 'responsible' ladies and gentlemen and entitled to know what was going on within their own hospital. They were also entitled to expect people to whom they paid a salary to co-operate in keeping them informed. In short, if I wanted to continue working at the Warneford I would give all information required.

And so it proved! Certain board members had a curiosity greater than I would have believed possible, and no personal detail was too trivial to be ignored, especially if the person concerned was known to the board member. I have often wondered what Warwickshire would have said could it have realised exactly how much became known to these people with every meeting. Talk about invasion of privacy!

I have also often asked myself what other course was open to me. I might have contacted the secretary of the British Medical Association and requested advice. Instinct, however, told me that the situation would eventually boil down to the simple issue of a junior person challenging his local establishment, and I had no illusions about any outcome under these circumstances. Not only would I be shopped, but I would probably end up by having to emigrate. Nor did I get comfort from my chief. Gerald, no doubt, had his own problems and could also appreciate my point of view, but he was identified with the board and presumably went along with how it reacted, so it was unlikely that he would side with me in a show-down. Not only could I not win, but I was not going to be allowed to win.

Coroners' courts were also a problem. I felt that they were frequently farcical, unnecessary, and angled towards covering up operations where 'judged in the public interest'. On one occasion I benefited from this myself and was grateful to the coroner for protection. Several men had died underground and I had been obliged to carry out the autopsies. Since I had never done such work before it was not surprising that when they were finally wound up I was not one bit further on towards establishing a diagnosis and I arrived at the coroner's court prepared to be exposed as a sham.

The question 'what was the exact cause of death' was expected, but my reply was sheer inspiration, and I could hardly believe that it was my own voice which replied: 'Death was due to the inhalation of noxious vapours.'

A counsel wrinkled his nose and had begun to frame a sentence beginning with the words 'noxious vapours' (which meant precisely nothing at all) when the coroner glanced at me sharply, half-smiled, and took charge. No one got a word in edgeways for fifteen minutes, after which, and still talking, he recorded that death had been due to the inhalation of noxious vapours, congratulated me on the precise manner in which my 'expert' evidence had been given and wound up the proceedings. I passed counsel in a nearby corridor and if looks could have killed I would have gone up in a column of smoke. For reasons of his own it had been desirable to establish which gas had been at fault, and now the whole thing would have to be approached from another angle.

The question of a (query) beautiful German spy also still intrigues me. She was a voluptuous brunette and admitted to the private wing suffering from a threatened abortion. She asked only one favour, that visitors reach her only by appointment, and I was amused to find that a Wing Commander clocked in at fourteen hundred hours precisely, a full colonel at seventeen hundred, and a naval commander at twenty-hundred.

She spoke English with an attractive accent which was difficult to place and said that she had been born of English parents in France. We became quite friendly and I enjoyed her company. She had some amusing stories of a famous English public school for girls and some slightly off-colour anecdotes about celebrities on holiday on the French Riviera. She aborted on her fourth day (I think) and spoke fluent German while going under the anaesthetic. She also swore in German when coming out of it. Next day I suggested, jokingly, that she must be 'one of these beautiful spies one reads about but who don't really exist' and we had a good laugh at the very idea. She then explained that when she had said 'born in France' she meant Alsace, and that the village in which her parents had lived for several years spoke German.

That same afternoon 'plain clothes men' arrived at the Warneford to see her and spoke with me for a few moments while I sent for a nurse to take them along to the private wing, but the bird had flown. Or at least she had disappeared. So far as I know she was never traced, though the police were coy about discussing the matter, and for all I know they may have picked her up within the hour. I forget her names, but I think she was called Marianne. Either that or Mary Anne. One part of me hopes that she managed to keep out of jail. She was very attractive but the question as to who had 'tipped her off' remained unsolved . . . to myself at least.

After Dunkirk, I was restless. One question only was uppermost in mind. When would I be called up? I enquired at length and was advised if I wanted to 'make myself more useful for the moment', to take a job in London. A week or two later I was accepted at Fulham Hospital in good time to see the first of the Blitz. We had a white house in Baron's Court Road and an Alsatian dog.

London was still enjoying life and the medical world had changed in few essentials. I met an assorted mixture of oddities at Fulham and I think especially of two family doctors who jointly operated a legal, foolproof, but amoral racket which was a fantastic money-spinner. One, call him A, practised, let us say, in Putney while the other, B, was for the sake of argument in West Ham, but they jointly rented premises in a world famous West End 'medical street' and A held sessions on Monday, Wednesday and Friday while B held court on Tuesday, Thursday and Saturday, each for 3 hours daily.

Both were actually seniors in general practices and partners coped with most of the routine work, but A's people would, whenever possible, advise a 'second opinion from a very brilliant fellow in Harley, or Wimpole or Whatever Street'. An appointment was then arranged for Tuesday, Thursday or Saturday, while B's staff, following the same guide lines, sent their people to the 'brilliant chap in Harley, Wimpole or Whatever Street' on Monday, Wednesday or Friday.

A 'saw' B's people.

B 'saw' A's people.

Neither were 'specialists' as the term is generally understood, but money rolled in, and on Sundays they separated the tens from the twenties. Both men are still alive, according to the current Medical Directory, and I have no wish to expose them.

For all I know they have mended their ways, but they introduced me to at least one of the various side-shows open to unscrupulous persons anxious to own their own Rolls Royce.

Knowledge made me cynical about *any* 'man in, say, "Harley Street" ' unless I had first checked his hospital appointments and career through the Medical Directory. How many people, realise, even today, that *anyone able to afford the rent* can set up as a Harley or Wimpole Street 'specialist'? The phrase means precisely nothing except that there is money around. Everything depends upon the status of the man who pays the rent.

One chief also introduced me to a clinic whose name I also hesitate to give, because, for all I know, things may also have changed. Let it suffice that in 1940 public rooms, suites, waiting-rooms, offices, corridors and entrance were lush as any five star ultra-continental hotel of the '70s. Maidservants and lay-girls sported tailored uniforms which would have been a credit to modern airline hostesses, but the operating suites had to be seen to be believed. A series of cubicles opened from a common corridor, and anaesthetists with others commuted freely from one theatre to the other. I have seen men walk out of a theatre polluted with pus from a foetid abscess and stroll in to another a few paces further along where a 'clean' operation of election was in progress, and where sepsis, by James Eric Paterson standards would have been inexcusable. I decided, after my first visit, that the circumstances could never arise when I would allow either Trudie or myself ever to have treatment in such a place. Yet it had a world-wide reputation. It was used by 'in-people' and 'now-personalities' not forgetting the glamour pussies, débutantes and stars 'of stage and screen'.

To say that I was disillusioned would have been the understatement of a century. I was appalled. The theatre lay-out would not have been tolerated in a slum district of Glasgow or Edinburgh. Yet it catered for the cream of the social cream.

It is also interesting to consider what manner of men worked there. Surely, I thought, they must have low standards if they were prepared to accept a superficial veneer of professionally useless sophisticated luxury, yet expose their patients to risk under circumstances perfectly conditioned to favour cross-infection. Yet some of the men involved cut a deal of ice. A few were rated as only slightly less than God, but John William Peden would not have given the theatres house-room within Kilmarnock Infirmary.

Fulham also taught me how London, far from being a 'city' as such is really an agglomeration of villages, each with its own traditions, dialect and history, and each with its special problems or interests. I began to accept it, not as a coherent entity, but as a polyglot collection of sub-tribes forced by circumstances to amalgamate into an over-crowded conurbation – which made an over-compensation element easy to understand! The wartime song *Maybe It's Because I'm a Londoner* did something to suggest that there *was* a London town, but my patients never, just never, came from London. They came from Stepney, or Dulwich, or Maida Vale, or Hammersmith and only a minority ever said that they came from London. Even so, a W.1 address is still worth paying for, and W.1 doctors were distinctly superior in their manner towards lesser lights from remote places like Bromley or Limehouse. They were united, however, in one thing. Scots, to them, were interesting curiosities. 'The Romans built a wall to keep you people out,' said one, 'and if they failed why should we succeed?' I was expected to drink whisky, wear kilts (not a kilt or the kilt, but kilts) and there was curiosity to know what was worn underneath. One man even asked me, when he saw a wedding photograph of myself in the kilt. 'Sa-a-ay! Anything worn under that?'

I could not resist an obvious reply. 'Nothing worn, sir. Everything's in perfect working order.'

To be a Scot in London was a greater advantage than being a Scot in Edinburgh. Londoners were generous, interested, and treated me kindly. They told amusing stories about how every top job in England was held by a Scot, and how they had a Scots grandparent or great-great-grandparent. Warwickshire had often made me feel like a country bumpkin, but Londoners could not have been nicer, even if they would not *allow* me to be BRITISH. It was extraordinary to be 'made' a Scot, because I had never thought very much about nationality. A man could not help where he was born, any more than he could help the colour of his skin. If I thought about it I was only vaguely aware

95

that I was a Caucasian born in Britain, so to have a Scottish 'thing' almost forced upon me was entertaining. I also discovered, from listening to the gossip of colleagues, that Scotland was a remote distant place where the Haggis flew in May and seldom bred in captivity; where clans awakened to the skirl of pipes and ladies from hell wielded battle axes. It was a misty land of stags, deer, whisky, black houses and lonely glens. It was a sort of mythical Nirvanah, a romantic ideal bespattered with phenomena like Celtic or Rangers football teams and young men who did not play cricket, a weirdy place of fairy folk, porridge and a road to the isles which somehow carried people over the sea to Skye.

So I discovered that there was no Britain except when thinking in patriotic terms. There were only 'the Lakes', the North East or the South West, the Home Counties or the Midlands, Cornwall or The North (Lincoln). And so far as certain consultants were concerned each had a fiscal value. Patients from the Home Counties and South West could 'pay'. Patients from the North East or The Midlands might be more doubtful propositions and have to be filtered into something less pricey than money-spinning snob clinics. As for patients from Scotland! Was there such a thing? The idea was good for a laugh – and we all laughed a great deal.

Life was a song: a blend of parties and theatres, nights in Soho and afternoons in The Park, an occasional visit to Westminster and visits to Kew or Richmond until the Blitz suddenly reminded us that we really were at war. Fulham had a rough time. The hospital was heavily bombed, and on one occasion the theatre in which I was operating was wrecked. Trudie walked in a few seconds later from the nearby shelter, but in time to hear the next bomb land outside and crack the theatre along two walls and across the ceiling.

The ball, so to speak, was over.

Next morning, when we were leaving the place, a five-inch sliver of hot shrapnel whistled between us and ripped open a sandbag beside her shoulder. It was all useful training for the weeks which lay ahead, and it was about this time that an aerial photograph of Rotterdam proved how her parents' home had been totally reduced to rubble during the bombardment of May

10th. Many months passed before we discovered that they were alive, yet never once did she complain, or increase my own problems by off-loading any of her anxieties in bouts of tantrums or temperament. In fact these blitz months became increasingly happy for us both. We were together more or less all the time and had placed our Alsatian in a safe house in the country. Trudie did whatever work she could in the hospital itself, and we were annoyed only that official bodies refused to use her for any form of service whatsoever because she was 'an alien by birth'.

I have often asked myself if British security has any dirt on some member of the van der Poest Clement family, because why else should she have been treated so high-handedly by *every* organisation to which she offered her services? In every case, for four-and-a-half years, they refused to use her after taking down her history, family name and address. No other explanation seems possible, yet the idea seems equally absurd. So far as I know every member of her extensive family are Anglophile and of such respectability that I would doubt if any of them have ever done anything even marginally shady in several generations. Be that as it may, Trudie was denied the right to serve in any official capacity anywhere, and that was that. The country's loss was my own gain.

German inability to hit Battersea Power Station and their tendency to hit Fulham Hospital instead finally destroyed its capacity to function, and by November the staff was re-posted. A chance meeting in Edinburgh with a civil servant from Saint Andrew's House then caused me to be diverted into a curious organisation called the Emergency Medical Service (E.M.S.).

Theory behind this was sound enough at first glance. Air-raids had been expected in the event of war breaking out, and 'temporary' hospitals were being built to cope. A number of smaller existing hospitals located in country districts were also involved in the scheme, and it was intended that junior specialists with 'higher' qualifications but limited field experience would staff such units under control of senior men over the age for service duties. It seemed that I fell into exactly this category. I had good paper qualifications but only limited experience, and my Edinburgh contact considered that, for the moment at least, I was ideal 'material' for the E.M.S. – especially since the Army now found itself back in Britain, but with no adequate hospital organisation. I gathered that the E.M.S. would, for the indefinite future, cope with service requirements plus any air-raid civilian casualties which could not be handled in the main centres. The work would be responsible and 'in the national interest'.

My first posting was to Stonehouse Hospital, Lanarkshire, with a visiting brief for Cleland and various other minor places in the same county, where it was difficult to believe that there was a war on. Hospital life was uncomplicated and for long I dealt more with routine civilian problems than either air-raid casualties or service men. We preserved dozens of eggs, to be bought for the asking at any farm. We ate well, lived well, and felt unhappy only because we both knew that somehow we had got on to the wrong conveyor belt. Trudie, it seemed, was an undesirable alien and I was destined to live a privileged life at home while drama unfolded elsewhere.

In May 1941, drama suddenly hit our own area when Rudolf Hess baled out to visit the Duke of Hamilton in an attempt to wind up the war – only a few miles from where we were living; and even fewer miles from Stonehouse Hospital.

The following weeks were fascinating, and it all began when the superintendent told me in confidence that Hess had injured his ankle on landing and that he, Smith, had been called out to give first aid. I was impressed, to say the least of it, and it sounded entirely possible. After all, Stonehouse *was* the nearest hospital. I also realised that Smith must have spoken out of turn, and was not surprised when he pressed me to promise that I would not repeat what he had told me. I was also interested in his impressions of Hess as a man, so I told only my wife, from whom I have never had any secrets, or hardly any, and that was that.

Some days later, however, a dentist told me in strictest confidence that Hess had landed badly after baling out, that his right knee had smacked against his jaw when he doubled up, and that several teeth had been damaged. The dentist, I discovered, had 'fixed him up' and I promised not 'to tell'. He too had interesting impressions of the man.

On that same evening an orthopaedic surgeon told me, also

under the seal of professional confidence, that Hess had broken an arm when landing and that he had been called in to cope. His impressions, understandably, got maximal audience response!

A week or so later a second orthopaedic surgeon whispered (in similar confidence) that Hess had dislocated his right hip on landing. In fact he had 'copped' a fracture dislocation, and the orthopod in question would never forget the occasion. First aid on the moors! A secret theatre session at a hospital whose name he wasn't allowed to disclose! Post-operative chest complications at some secret medical hide-out deep in the country: if not underground! And, of course, impressions! All in all he told the best story.

But why, I kept asking myself, did these rather senior men so much want to impress a still junior person like myself? I found it all very odd. Yet there was an unexpected sequel. Several years later, when assisting Professor Lennie, the gynaecologist, I told him the story. He could understand how I felt. 'But think about me,' he added. 'Some of them told me the same sort of story, and I had to listen and let them believe I was impressed, when all the time I was actually in charge of the man.' And then I remembered. Lennie had, indeed, been commandant at Buchanan Castle during the Hess period and Hess must have been under his care. I still recall that far-away glint in the professor's eyes when he explained how dearly he would have liked to tell the sensation-seekers what liars they really were.

It is just possible that Dr Smith was involved on the periphery of the Hess incident. He would have been a fairly obvious man to call in during such an emergency and I give him the benefit of the doubt. But the rest! Dear me! So I learned yet another lesson which has been confirmed again and again: men who feel themselves to be quite small will do almost anything to promote their public image. Especially when they believe it will be impossible to disprove their case.

The Hess episode apart, our Lanarkshire year was almost incident free, other than the occasional drama which broke in Motherwell Fever Hospital. The Superintendent, Doctor Reid, was attached to his ancient pipe and to his very ancient dog (or bitch). The little creature was rheumaticky, foul-breathed, easily irritated but still curious about everything. The two were inseparable, and would jointly visit my theatre during operating sessions. Even granted that there was usually plenty of pus around, that was still no excuse for the four-footed friend sniffing my bloody boots or putting his nose against suspect swabs. Yet the old man was clearly surprised when I suggested that the dog might be left 'outside', and it was easy to see how his mind ticked. Junior surgeons were still two a penny, even in wartime, but there was only one dog. If he had to make a choice it was easy to guess which of us would survive, and by and large I agreed with him. Our own dogs were beloved, and our two Kerry Blue Terriers were undisputed lords of all they surveyed.

The diphtheria incident, however, was more personal. I had read about similar situations in books but never imagined one would come my own way. A child's throat became obstructed by membrane late one evening. There was an immediate need to insert a tube into its wind-pipe below the obstruction or it would die, and so Motherwell Fever Hospital gave me yet one more 'first', but matters did not go according to plan. For reasons which escape me now, but which must have been commanding, it became necessary to do something more drastic and I sucked up the membrane through a tube into my own mouth. When the throat was as clear as possible we waited for a little while, and when the physicians judged that the child was fit for tracheotomy I performed the operation, though maximally preoccupied about the diphtheria bugs which must still be in my own throat. I had never suffered from the disease, and so far as I knew I had never been immunised against it.

I tried to play things cool, and waited until after the inevitable coffee before asking if Doctor Reid would now give me a shot of anti-diphtheritic serum. He looked surprised and asked why. I became self-conscious but tried to explain that I was now at risk of infection myself, which amused him greatly and he became off-hand about the whole business. Diphtheria, I gathered, was not likely to affect a doctor, even if he had gargled with membrane and swallowed countless million bugs. An acid conversation followed until eventually, but with no grace, he gave me the shot. 'You've gone down in my estimation,' he said. 'Can't think why you young chaps get scared of a thing like that.'

I also commuted to Hairmyres Hospital and was able, from

time to time, to watch Bruce Dick perform some of the earliest heart operations carried out in Scotland. It was a hairy experience at times and gave no hint of advances which were to follow within a quarter of a century. Bruce Dick was a hefty fellow who vaguely reminds me of the late George Sanders. His textbook of surgical pathology, written jointly with Professor Illingworth of Glasgow University, was one of the better medical books produced during my early years and partly responsible for enabling me to pass the Fellowship examination. Yet I found him more than usually unapproachable. He was, I suppose, one of the smaller giants and what the Scots call a man of parts. It is curious that, although the Illingworth–Dick book is superb, neither of the authors appealed to me as men.

Hairmyres Hospital, East Kilbride, had a vaguely military atmosphere, but, that apart, there was little around to remind us that there was a war on, and my continuing sense of guilt at holding down a cushy job (even if grossly underpaid) made me writhe with shame. It also made me agitate for transfer, and I was sent to Bangour in the autumn of 1941. Bangour was a large Emergency Medical Service Hospital some ten miles west of Edinburgh, and we rented a furnished bungalow in Corstorphine. The owner was at sea and was drowned a year or so later. His wife disappeared from our ken, but the house produced one major surprise when Trudie opened a drawer in a chest laid aside for our own use, and discovered a collection of superb Japanese pornographic pictures, either prints or worked with minute stitches on silk. They were, literally, the first such things either of us had ever seen and childhood training told me that I ought to put on an act of being horrified. This I did, for a day or two, and until we had come to our senses, after which the subject was digested with more consideration. Memory of that original 'pretence-routine' became important years later when I heard my peers protesting about the so-called pornography of the late '60s and '70s. Every instinct, plus personal experience, told me they were phoney, and that given half a chance of being able to enjoy a pornographic episode they would dive in up to the neck. Though I also knew that few would have the courage, since they would always be afraid of being found out unless able to indulge under a mask of 'research'. However, these Japanese panels were an important part of my own education and I regret only that we did not hold on to one or two.

The drawer also held a number of very personal but infinitely sad little things. There was, for example, a crisp curl of what looked like pubic hair gummed on to a square of glossy cardboard and with neat writing on top. 'I cut this off in my bath. Caress yourself with it if you are lonely, darling. All my love.'

This was my first really big step forward in terms of sex education, proving as it did the existence of those vast areas of thought which were publicly denied by all elders of my own tribe. It even seemed sensational that a woman could speak or write so frankly about sex, or show her sensuality and affection so beautifully. The incident became even more sad when we eventually discovered that the couple had never again met after separation at the beginning of the war. There were also a few still unsolved problems. Why had she left these things in that drawer? How many others had she sent? Or had she sent none at all, and were these only abortive ideas which she had been frightened to post with all the implicit censorship risks? We met her only once. She was small, plumpish, rising forty, and apparently very 'ordinary'. It was good to know that below an apparently conventional, almost frumpish exterior, there was a spirit capable of such awareness and sensitivity. I began, from then on, to outgrow the hundred and one tabus which had been engrained deep into my own outlook by an inhibited society.

I also remember Bangour Hospital because of one incident involving really high drama. A patient had been admitted suffering from that lethal killer, gas-gangrene, but an early sulphonamide preparation was available and given in full dosage. Response was swift and convincing. Sir Henry Wade arrived on a routine visit and was shown the case. He was impressed beyond words, and it took a great deal to rob Henry of words. Every available nurse was then summoned to share his experience and he demonstrated for an hour, reminiscing about gas-gangrene during the First World War and how impotent he had felt at being unable to do anything.

He returned next day to find the patient still improving, and again called in as many of the staff as possible. He was incoherent with excitement, and Henry was not a man to show deep emotion easily, but next day he almost wept, and I could see actual tears in his eyes when he checked the man over in detail, took a deep breath and said to the people around. 'Ladies and gentlemen, you have seen a great miracle. It is like divine intervention.'

Such was my own introduction to wonder-drugs which are now taken for granted. Every time I find a patient who is off-hand or careless I wish so much that I could show him the past and prove exactly what miracles have indeed been worked during this antibiotic era. I am grateful that I was privileged to share Sir Henry's sense of mystery when he said 'you have seen a great miracle'.

Another attempt to be released from the Emergency Medical Service was thumbed down because of the Direction of Labour Order (or so I was told), but it also brought greater responsibility with my transfer to Woodend-Oldmill Hospitals, Aberdeen. These local authority institutions had been expanded by many hundreds of beds and were serving a mixed bag of civilians, allied forces and prisoners of war.

Brigadier William Anderson had a mysterious briefing as overall chief on the service side but retained a special interest in performing thoracoplasties on the civilian. Andrew Fowler, Gordon Bruce and Sidney Davidson, all consultant surgeons in the Royal, had their own E.M.S. beds and at first made regular visits, until, eventually, ever-increasing responsibility was delegated to myself.

Aberdeen is where I really found my feet and became less of a public menace. We rented a granite bungalow in Kings Road, kept two Afghan hounds and settled down the better for discovering, through the Red Cross, that Trudie's family was all alive even after the bombing of Rotterdam.

My first meeting with Sidney Davidson paved the way to an easy relationship. I had walked into his theatre at Woodend while he was removing a bullet from a man's thigh. It was lodged half inside the femoral artery and when pulled out blood almost hit the ceiling. His assistant failed to compress the artery properly from above and I took over. Sidney had his own problems and I was lucky 'at my end'. When haemorrhage was finally under control he wrinkled his brows. 'I don't know who the hell you are but I'm glad to see you.'

I could not have got off to a better start, and three years slipped past under such ideal conditions that I was black ashamed of my good fortune. So much so, indeed, that I repeatedly tried to get off the hook, but was always told that the E.M.S. took first priority. I was also continually reminded that I was unable to resign because Direction of Labour was still in operation. However, every effort to get into the services, any service, did morale good, and for a few months I was more resigned – though the situation always did rankle.

It was when I was in a sorry-for-myself humour that I decided to investigate in depth a technique which I had started in 1938 when confronted with the need to repair an enormous rupture in a patient with grossly defective muscles. The possibility of reinforcing 'weak' areas on the abdominal wall with a skin plaque had earlier been in my mind, and I had used the idea when it became obvious that there was little hope of any routine approach being able to control that particular problem. The hernia had developed through an enormous operation scar and I sutured a skin graft under maximal tension to every possible anchorage around. The result was satisfactory, and had remained satisfactory. I had then, from time to time, used the same technique for repair of various kinds of large rupture, but it had become important to work out the exact fate of the skin. Did it undergo any change? And if so, what? I had been able, on two occasions, to operate upon a person for another condition many months after a whole skin graft had been on-laid to repair a central hernia, and study of biopsies from these grafts had encouraged me to believe that the skin did actually convert into a stout plaque of fibrous tissue, that it was not 'rejected' and that it did not undergo any change which would suggest risk of malignancy or other complication. I decided, in Aberdeen, to pursue this work and to do a series of hernia repairs using my skin graft technique and eventually write up the findings as a monograph. John Smith, superintendent of the City Hospital, won permission for me to conduct certain experiments in the animal laboratories under his control, and I became licensed for vivisection.

Vivisection is a dirty eleven letter word, so it is well to explain that the whole affair is strictly supervised. First of all, there are grades of licence, each permitting only certain types of work to be carried out, and those only upon certain types of animal. The authorities who issue the licences have also to be satisfied about the nature of the experiments proposed, the capacity and credibility of the applicant and the potential of his activities. If a licence is granted, inspectors make spot checks at surprising hours to confirm not only the well-being of the animals but that the record of each has been accurately written up. Detail must be exact, and every experiment or test must be recorded at the time and on the spot.

I slipped up in this on one occasion and failed to complete a case report on one rabbit, having been called back to Woodend to deal with a surgical emergency. It was unfortunate that inspectors arrived early next morning. The rocket delivered was shattering – so shattering, in fact, that I was never again careless.

It should also be understood that I love animals. In fact, I love all animals including gnu, duck-billed platypuses and even skunks, but love only a minority of all human beings whom I have met, so it follows that my rabbits were gently handled. Anaesthetics were given as though to a nervous teenager, and few died. At worst they each had two operations: one to apply what came to be known as my 'whole skin grafts', and a second to have portions removed together with adjacent tissue. Scarring was minimal and they were eventually given to pet shops or to children who also cared.

The animal experiments also entailed an enormous amount of microscopy since every graft had to be studied in serial section and hundreds of sections photographed after suitable preparation. Meanwhile I had to write up my findings and consider how they applied to the human subject. To round matters off, the end point was publication of a book, *The Surgery of Abdominal Hernia* (Arnolds, Edinburgh, 1948). It was well received and is my own single, small, contribution to surgical progress as opposed to medical or general practice.

I became increasingly curious about the whole field of my own general ignorance and kept wondering whether or not I really knew enough even to pass my final examinations again, though there was one easy enough way to find out. Glasgow has a very old Faculty; older, in fact, than either the London or Edinburgh Colleges of Surgeons, but then known as the Royal Faculty of Physicians and Surgeons of Glasgow (R.F.P.S.G.). Candidates were allowed to sit entrance examinations only twice and pass percentage was low.

I decided that it would be good for my soul to confirm my worst expectations and attempt the Glasgow Fellowship, though it was necessary for my purpose not to prepare myself in any way for the examination, but to sit it as a routine check upon my everyday reservoir of knowledge. The whole business, however, proved tiresome, difficult and stress-making. I became irritated with most of the examiners during the vivas, and with myself for having got involved once again in the examination atmosphere. Believe me, no one was more surprised than myself when I passed, and became, to my astonishment, a Fellow of the Royal Faculty of Physicians and Surgeons of Glasgow. Some years ago the Faculty became a Royal College, and Fellows were given the right to choose whether they wished to retain their old style or go modern and become a Fellow of the Royal College of Surgeons (or Physicians) (Glasgow). I opted to keep the old style, and that was that.

Meanwhile, in Aberdeen, life was more or less perfect. Trudie had at last managed to secure some sort of job, but even in Aberdeen long invisible official hands still seemed to reach out, and 'meals on wheels' was all we could contrive. It was exasperating, but we made the best of it. I arranged concerts to entertain the troops, of whom we now had large numbers. We went to the theatre at least once a week and had endless exercise in Hazelhead Woods, a place with an interesting history which we did not discover until we had named our first home Hazelhead House in 1946. The fact is that the estate, which is magnificent, was bequeathed to Aberdeen City Council for use by the public. The City fathers, however, felt that the original name 'lacked dignity' and switched to Hazelhead from Burnieboozle. What a word! And how odd that even city councillors, whom I have seldom found to be either forward-thinking or gifted with much initiative, should have thumbed it down. Burnieboozle is tailor-made for publicity.

The venereal disease unit at Woodend first introduced me to the new, and extremely important problem of resistance to anti-biotic drugs. Gonorrhoea responded dramatically to 'new' tablets, then known as 'M. and B.'. A black market in sulphonamides followed, and when it became clear that acute gonorrhoea would dry up within forty-eight hours or less, M. and B. was able to buy anything. Eight tablets was reward enough for a Tunisian prostitute or the sister of an Egyptian shoe-shine boy. Servicemen took tablets prophylactically, but in low dosage, and it was some time before it was discovered that symptoms could then be masked and eventual complications become more severe. Even worse, it took time to prove that unless a full course was taken *the infecting organism would become resistant to later doses*. Worse still! If transmitted to another person treatment would be unsatisfactory. Catastrophe of all catastrophes, however, there were already 'strains' of gonococci which were insensitive to at least one of the new drugs.

This problem of resistant infections has plagued medicine ever since, and when I became a family doctor I was continually riled by the carelessness shown by too many patients towards almost any drug given. Their attitude to dosage was slap-happy, and more resistant strains were generated every month in probably every practice in Britain through patients' combined indifference, carelessness or ignorance. The situation would have become impossible and the age of wonder-drugs reduced to a few years but for continued research by manufacturing chemists who somehow contrived to keep a pace or two ahead of events. *Nor was any national campaign launched to inform and train patients.*

Attitudes of staff to the venereal disease patients were also interesting. Where, during peace time, certain women would, I am certain, have damned the men as licentious and immoral outcasts, they came to believe that war-time V.D. was 'different' and somehow excusable. I was eventually to discover how some would never accept that V.D. acquired during the tension of peace may be equally excusable. I was also reminded of the old medical chestnut that 'only priests, clergymen and doctors ever get V.D. from towels or lavatory seats' – another way of saying that venereologists will sometimes allow churchmen or doctors a peg upon which to hang some claim to self-respect, but that *all* V.D. is always acquired through direct contact, flesh to flesh.

Changing to a more agreeable subject, and one so far removed from the venereologists as is the moon from green cheese, Mary Garden, easily Scotland's most famous-ever prima-donna, lived near Aberdeen, although her name was more familiar to New York Metropolitan Opera-lovers than to her own people. I met her on several occasions, and she had a greater presence and more remarkable style than almost any other woman I have known. She 'projected', even on an Aberdeenshire moor, and her complexion would have been envied by many teenagers. She loved to say that 'the best place to start a career was at the top', 'a hint at her own break when, with both principal and under-study sick in Paris, a desperate producer discovered that a reliable singing professor had trained a Scots girl who showed promise. She was an over-night Parisian sensation as *Norma* and never looked back, returning to Scotland only occasionally to keep in contact and feel that she still 'belonged'. Her particular protégé was a Canadian cowboy, Mel Fengsted, who won the Calgary Rodeo championship on three successive years – or so we were given to understand – and Mel, while convalescing from a long-term problem taught me some of his own mysteries. They made an odd couple, the gangling cowboy and the patrician prima-donna.

From time to time we also had an air-raid alert, but they seldom meant anything and we all tended to become blasé, until, one evening I saw an aircraft fly at near roof top level along Kings Gate, where we lived, with two machine guns knocking chips from side-walks and walls. It was curtain up to a sharp raid. Several people were killed, and my night passed at Woodend coping with casualties. I was interrupted only when Andrew Fowler, one of my chiefs, entered the theatre holding a piece of shrapnel. He looked surprised and was in casual clothes, but I remember his remark verbatim. 'I was in the garage when that damn't thing came through the roof. Hit the car and stotted on to the bonnet. And it newly sprayed last week!'

Andrew felt deeply about his cars and cherished them like babes, but I figure he must have been mildly shocked to have motored two or three miles simply to tell me what had happened. He never referred to it again and the incident remains a pointless mystery, except, possibly, to prove how strong silent men can be jerked out of low profile poses by a sudden shock.

Our Woodend-Oldmill lives were also complicated by a different and very unexpected situation, and I cannot imagine why I ever came to say what I did. It happened, however, that I went to hospital one morning an hour or so before dawn to cope with an acute appendix and my car had to pass along an avenue of trees and skirt lawns flanked by bushes. Next day during luncheon when asked by the superintendent if it had been 'cold during the night' I said, without thinking, 'goodness yes. I even saw a ghost near the rhododendrons and went gooseflesh all over'.

It was a heedless spontaneous remark, especially from one who would not have been seen dead in a ditch with a ghost, but it provoked immediate reaction and I learned that all present, from the superintendent down, believed the hospital to be haunted by a 'grey lady'. Two practical down-to-earth-and-no-nonsense lady doctors had seen her several times. The superintendent himself had seen her more than once. Three or four men had also watched her either walk through walls or stroll on the lawn. They had all pledged themselves not to mention the business to 'other people' in order to avoid 'panic', but were anxious to talk when they discovered that I seemed to have joined the club. Nor would protests that I had 'only been joking' satisfy them. They were convinced that I was trying to reassure and would not wear it for a moment.

The grey lady became a recurring topic of conversation. She was seen by several sisters, and eventually by a few hard-headed patients, but judge my own surprise when I saw her myself! It was during a late night call and there was good visibility. There was no mist, and a touch of frost had etched the trees clear against a lovely winter sky. The moon was bright, but casting no peculiar shadows, yet the lady strolled out from some bushes a score or so yards away and moved across the lawns towards the hospital. She was in full view for at least two minutes and I can swear on oath that she was dressed like an old-time matron. Her features were pale but those of an early middle-aged woman. I could see her ankles and she *walked*. She did not 'glide', or 'float' or 'progress' or 'move'. She walked. Period. And she walked right through the front wall of the hospital to the left of the entrance door: which meant that she entered the superintendent's office direct. And I was not afraid. Nor was I drunk, because I have never been drunk in my life. Nor was I drugged, because drugs do not figure either. Nor was I cold, 'broken out in chill sweat' or emotionally upset. She was a 'nice', grey lady, and thereafter I thought of her with capital letters. She became my Grey Lady, and although I never saw her again I still find it difficult to reject the evidence, especially since other people involved were mostly stark realists and some of them downright cynical. The Club had no doubting Thomases and we were almost sorry, when, by 1945, she seemed to have deserted us, and was not, so far as I know, seen again.

She was my own first 'ghost'.

The second appeared years later in a small house we bought in Perthshire, and I found her, late one night, sitting, in period dress, on a Georgian wine cooler. She looked sad and there were tears in her eyes. She was also young and I thought I had never seen anyone so wretched. I was a little off-put, though only for a moment or two. When I switched on the electric light she was still there, but standing between us was our favourite Afghan, Sheba, who had died of old age some time earlier. She looked

110

young again and in her prime, her teeth were magnificent and her slowly wagging tail made me feel good. Sheba even smiled, a thing she often did in life on this dimension, and she was able to make me understand that I had nothing to fear. I brewed some coffee and both Sheba and the sad lady disappeared while I was drinking it.

Next morning my wife wakened, tired and ill at ease. She said that she had had a dream, that Sheba had been to see her, that the bitch had 'become young again', had lovely teeth and was smiling.

'Explain THAT if you can,' I say to doubting Thomases.

I never actually saw the last ghost of whom I have personal knowledge. I had, years later, patients in a council house who were plagued by this particular apparition. The couple had married against the wishes of the girl's mother. When she died they 'acquired' her house and shortly afterwards the mother's shade appeared at the bottom of their bed night after night. The man's health broke under the strain and cure was finally worked only after I had persuaded the housing authorities to settle them elsewhere. Nor was this a complicated 'fiddle' to get another house. The second one, from every angle, was less desirable than the first, but they grabbed it with both hands and the ghost withdrew.

So I believe in ghosts, and my brother believes in ghosts, though we do not encourage them. We are not spiritualists and we do not dabble in, or particularly study the occult. We simply accept that certain people may be able to appreciate a presence and even see it. In other words, we leave ghosts alone if they leave us alone.

Grey Lady notwithstanding, Oldmill-Woodend kept us all busy, and new problems began to develop when we received prisoners of war. Some were arrogant, and on one occasion a seventeen-year-old youth threw a plate of custard into the face of the young nurse who served him. I reacted without thinking and signed to two other nurses, who were passing with loaded trays, to come to the bedside. I then let him have a plate of custard slam on each cheek and registered two bulls. One plate slightly bruised his forehead and action was threatened. A complaint, indeed, was lodged against me, and Brigadier Anderson descended from on high to cope. He was an unpredictable character, though I figured that whatever action he might have to take officially he would sympathise in private, but he only heard me out and grinned. 'Relax. Can't have these bloody Krauts doing that tae the wee lassies, or next time it'll be rape.'

Later that afternoon he invited me to join him on a visit to Aberdeen Royal where he wanted a word with his old friend, F. K. Smith, who was still in active practice as consultant surgeon. F.K. was doing a full ward round with all the trimmings, students formed a tail, and there was that hushed silence which is (or was) always associated with state visits from the Chief. But F.K. was unhappy and as William Anderson and I listened to him taking a case history we began to understand why. The patient probably had a fistula between bowel and stomach, but simply could not understand what F.K. was driving at when he asked questions like: 'Now tell me, is your breath ever foul?' Or 'How about taste? Do you still relish your wife's cooking?'

William eventually stepped forward, and in a loud, clear voice said with a broad Aberdeenshire accent: 'Hey, mon. Div ye fart froo yer moo?'*

The man's eyes lit up with immediate understanding and he half smiled. 'Aye, mon. An' shit too.'

'See,' said William triumphantly. 'A gastro-colic fistula, Fred. Why don't you learn to speak the language?'

It was a delightful little experience which must have proved for all time to the students that there is still a place for understanding the vernacular.

Aberdeen's consultant psychiatrist, Douglas MacAlman, was slowly becoming a personal friend. He was a man of distinction and understanding, who eventually launched the first post-war Chair of Psychiatry at Leeds University, but from time to time I found myself opening up a little over dinner at the Club or our own home, and Douglas became attentive. I had begun to have dreams again, and in particular I often found myself doing difficult block dissections of neck glands, stripping tissue from carotid arteries and jugular vein, and watching the great vessels throbbing under my fingers. This type of dream frequently

* Aberdeenshire dialect. 'Say, man. Do you pass bowel gas through your mouth!'

recurred, but always ended in the same way as I accidentally cut an artery and woke up while blood spurted over my clothes. They were frightening dreams and I wakened cold, perspiring, and reaching for my wife's arms. I also began to realise that Douglas was occasionally pumping me about my past history, and, late in 1944 he had a serious conversation. He said that my parents had been foolish in forcing me into medicine and even more foolish to have virtually ordered me into surgery. He added something which surprised me when he explained that no surgeon could be happy in his work unless he had a greater-than-normal sadistic component in his psyche and that he was confident I had much less of this than average. He then urged me to quit surgery as soon as might be practicable, thought that if I persisted I might well head for an anxiety condition or re-active depression, and argued that I was more suited either to an academic life or to some totally different type of career as a 'loner'. Meanwhile he thought that we should have a meal to-gether every few weeks and that I should keep him posted. He rated my assault on the German youth as an excuse to aggress against a symbol of the 'patient situation' which kept me busy with a knife, and predicted that history might repeat itself. He said that Trudie had probably saved me from some sort of crisis because of her serenity, love and awareness of my situation, and he enquired about my brother.

Alistair was then almost twenty, and following in my own footsteps, but much had happened during his early life which eventually became important. Craig Borland in particular had continued to be concerned by the possessiveness of our mother, and by the virtually boundless ambitions of our father. He believed that the youth would become anti-social as he grew older unless he was liberated from apron strings which seemed to be forged from high-tension steel. He had at last interfered directly and been finally responsible for our parents agreeing that Alistair would leave home and go to boarding school in Edinburgh.

I do not remember my brother ever expressing any particular wish to follow any particular career during his early teens, but it was taken for granted by everyone that he would become a doctor. Alistair was, and still is a sensitive person with a strong independent streak which makes him resent invasion of privacy, interference in his affairs, advice from others or suggestion that he is unable to cope. No one could have guessed that within twenty-odd years of graduation he would have quit medicine and shown sufficient capacity as an author to have become President of the Scottish Branch of International P.E.N., be recipient of at least one literary prize, have his works translated into seven or more languages, receive a £1,000 award from the Arts Council, and have written several radio plays. Or that he would suffer from that rare Royal Free Hospital Virus Infection which disturbs work out-put and tends to promote difficult environmental situations. Or that his marriage would be broken. Given a return to health he may be entering a productive period which could become significant.

The fact remained, however, that in 1944 I had my own problems, and was wondering how soon I could get off the hook. Douglas MacAlman argued that only an unjustified personal guilt sense made me undertake the enormous load of work which had become routine and that I was forcing myself to undergo penance for thoughts which I knew to be disloyal to my parents. However, I discovered that I was not the only local quack with emotional problems. Three close associates and colleagues, whose personalities I greatly envied, were all attending a psychiatrist weekly and had only adjusted with difficulty to routine living. Yet they *appeared* to be so composed, affable, relaxed and suave that I had actually envied them. One sublimated at least part of his tensions as a pianist and aggravated another set of problems by failing to reach concert standard. A second opted into general practice, married an agreeable girl and used his personality to sell a bedside manner which would have reassured Hitler himself. But he did adjust and the new life suited him. The third, a man of considerable authority, became more thin-lipped with every passing month, more taciturn with every year, and finally withdrew to the south where a contented family life helped to compose his own particular problems.

Ever since my Aberdeen days I have been suspicious of all men and most women who appear to be abnormally relaxed or tension free. They are usually seething volcanoes of neurosis and I prefer mild extroverts who 'aggress' normally like the rest of mankind. In fact, my most successful 'cure' was a woman with a broken marriage who became transformed within weeks of getting a job driving an earth moving machine. Nothing, she said, gave her more satisfaction than to rumble towards a house and smash it to smithereens. Her marriage took on a new lease of life and was happy for years until she changed her job. I then advised her husband to buy up the leavings of china or pottery at house sales or from junk shops and advised his wife to break a plate or smash a cup every time she felt uptight. That also worked, and is still working. They have, indeed lived semi-happily ever after.

Some people, it seems, MUST give expression to their aggressive instincts.

Christmas, 1944 saw Oldmill with an increasing number of German prisoners. I had heard them practising carols and took my wife to that same ward late on Christmas Eve when the N.C.O. in charge greeted us with stiff formality. Would his men please sing *Still the Night*, I asked?

Orders were snapped out with a zip which reminded me of the 1936 Danzig scene. His men snapped to attention and, standing rigidly with hands by their sides, sang like King's College choristers. It was unforgettable. We could see our own pine-woods dusted with frost outside the windows, a clear sky with a few high, scudding clouds, coldly platinum under a brilliant moon, and reflections of tinsel from Christmas trees in other wards. The Germans had made simple decorations, and pictures of their women stood on each bedside locker. The atmosphere slowly thawed and they became more friendly. Discipline relaxed, and as Trudie moved round, speaking to them in their own language or reminiscing about holidays in the Harz Mountains or along the Rhine, they became almost happy. More carols followed and we ended with a repeat of *Stille Nacht*.

By contrast, a month or so later a new admission to that same ward refused a life-saving blood transfusion 'unless it was German blood'. Since this was not possible on several counts he was allowed to die, and as he was a minor war criminal this was probably a mercy.

At around that same time a group of Free French soldiers managed to kidnap two Germans from another ward and

115

attempted to hang them in their own. I arrived by chance in the middle of the night, but in time to cut the Germans down alive, though by tacit consent none of us, not even the Germans, said anything to the hospital superintendent, and I still take off my hat to men who were able to pin-point wanted enemies under hospital conditions, court-martial them in the middle of the night and set up a hanging routine without disturbing even the nurse supposed to be on duty. I suspect that she was kept pre-occupied by a dashing young man, who had already scored several successes with the staff, many of whom were either V.A.D.s or part-timers. His technique was completely simple. He asked the same question of every girl who interested him, and scored, or so he claimed, a high rate of success: around seventy per cent, he thought. The plea 'Darling girl! Will you please play fukey-fuk with a poor soldier boy' worked, he said, like a charm.

The war was beginning to wind up and I made a trip to London, determined, somehow, to get Trudie into the organisation in which she was most interested. Fortunately, the Save the Children Fund was enthusiastic, preparations were being made to send teams abroad and Trudie's languages were invaluable. In the event, she reached Rotterdam within two days of liberation and loaded with goodies. So far as I was concerned, fresh efforts to get into the Services continued to be thwarted and my E.M.S. work still took priority. Work load rose rapidly, then slowly began to fall as armies moved forward into Europe and centres of activity moved away from our area. I also discovered that E.M.S. personnel were going to be called into the Services to release doctors who had done a stint of several years, and I was astonished. It seemed amoral to direct very young doctors into the Emergency Medical Service at the beginning of a war and then push them into uniform when the thing was almost over. None of us in the E.M.S. had tried to dodge the column, we had completed the questionnaire early in '39 or late '38 and offered to do service at home or abroad, so what manner of fools would we look if we went into uniform when there was no longer any danger and no longer any war?

Douglas MacAlman was sympathetic. It was, he said, only a rumour. Chances were that nothing would happen, but I was due to take a week's leave and he advised me to get on with it. I was not impressed. Instinct told me that trouble lay ahead, and with it an eyeball-to-eyeball confrontation with the Organisation.

Nor was I wrong! A telegram ordering me to report to Edinburgh Castle reached me when in Skye, and I had a 'temperament' in Sligachan Hotel. The situation was outrageous. I would emerge as a yellow-bellied coward. I had tried for years to get out of the E.M.S. – and had been thwarted. Not even Trudie had been allowed the sort of responsibilities which she had gone after right from the beginning of the war. I would not be able to hold my head up in public, or with our unborn children if this lot went through, and if it was the last thing I did I decided to try to get as much publicity as possible to expose a development which was an affront to professional men who were now victims of a situation not of their own making.

I told Douglas all this – and more – over the phone, went to Edinburgh on schedule and was filtered off into a side-room where a pale-faced officer grilled me. Our discussion was blunt. I said all that had to be said and a good deal more, and I remember that I was in a white-hot temper as he asked question after question which seemed to reflect upon my own personal courage or moral integrity. The interview went on for over an hour, at the end of which he told me that he was a consultant psychiatrist, that Douglas MacAlman had been in contact with him and that he was going to advise I be rejected for military service. He added that Douglas was of the same opinion and suggested that I withdraw from hack surgery to concentrate upon an academic approach. He further said that I was suffering from a chronic anxiety state and that I would hear no more about H.M. Forces.

Douglas had often held forth on what he called the sadistic component within all surgeons, claiming that every surgical operation not only involved the surgeon in a legal physical assault upon a patient, but ended by leaving a scar upon the body. He argued that no man could emotionally accept this sort of life unless one part of him was able to rationalise the situation and make himself believe that the assault, plus scar, was a small price to pay for cure of an important physical problem to which there was no other approach. Yet he maintained that no surgeon could stand up to this way of living unless, subconsciously, the assault and the scar satisfied a way-deep-down sadistic need.

Douglas also argued that I had undergone a major personality change after marrying Trudie, that her serenity had gone far to affect myself and that her gentleness had removed any possible bias towards such legalised sadistic outlets or patterns. It followed, he said, that surgery could, for myself, involve only conflict, and that I must get away from scalpels. He underlined that there was not a trace of psycho-pathology in my make-up and that there was nothing to be ashamed of in my situation. It was, he maintained, proof of a real sensitivity towards life and a new sensibility about standards of values.

All of which ran through my mind when I heard the verdict in Edinburgh Castle. The 'anxiety state' was simply a 'label'. Behind it I could detect the hand of Douglas MacAlman, the one man alive who knew my emotional history in detail. The psychiatrist's words left me cold, even although I knew that at long last I was finally free of the E.M.S. and with licence to angle into a different manner of living.

Yet it was a hollow victory. I would have preferred to refuse a commission and do a jail stretch so that publicity might at least lead to some sort of enquiry into the future of colleagues in the same position as myself. I had even said as much to Douglas before going to Edinburgh, and I suspected that this was the Organisation's way of keeping my mouth shut. Once again I could not win and Authority had seen to it that I would not be allowed to win. Anything I said would get low credit ratings since it came from a person rejected by the Forces on psychiatric grounds. No matter how much I agitated it would be officially attributed to a 'mental condition', and I was tabbed for life as a 'head case' if ever I tried to tilt against the Establishment. My goose was cooked. Anyone who cared to denigrate me could have the time of their lives, and open season for shooting down Mair would begin if I annoyed top people enough to matter.

Brigadier Anderson, who was also familiar with my history, was only amused. 'Prove you're sane, then,' he said. 'Prove I'm sane. Prove Montgomery or Churchill are sane. What are you belly-aching about? The whole world is daft. Meanwhile you've got an anxiety condition, and since a consultant psychiatrist said so, it must be so. That's the official line, though they're all liars, so get off my back and stop being difficult. The next case is yours.'

A few weeks later I saw an advertisement in the *British Medical Journal*, applied for the post, and left Aberdeen after more than three formative years to become Senior Assistant to the Professorial Unit in Durham University and Newcastle-upon-Tyne Royal Victoria Hospital, a position which the Americans more properly call Associate Professor. Professor Barclay was my chief and life became more tranquil. It was the academic ivory tower said to be more suited to my temperament.

Professor Barclay was small, modest and unassuming. He was also reassuring, competent and kind. His successor, Herbert Bentley, was a go-getting thruster with a panache which appealed to some, and a flair for teaching which was impressive. Above all, it was a privilege to sit at the feet of Professor Grey-Turner, one of the all-time 'greats'. He was then elderly and had retired from the chair but he still kept in touch as Emeritus, and, even more important, kept us in touch with what was happening behind the scenes elsewhere. He had become something of a senior medical politician. He was interested in my Whole Skin Graft experiments and, like my father, a stout believer that 'a pat on the back pushes a man further than a kick on the pants'.

Nevertheless, the personality I best remember and most respect from Newcastle days is Andrew Logan. When I first met him he was a tall, shy, gangling man with an apologetic manner who was said to show greater-than-usual promise as a surgeon. He told me how much he was interested in thoracic surgery and hinted at a few of his theories. Neither of us could then have guessed that he was destined to develop Edinburgh's thoracic unit, or to perform the first heart and lungs transplant. Death was due to the effect of paraquat, as most of the world must remember, and Andrew Logan courted no publicity. Yet he is one of the greatest giants of our times.

9 NEWCASTLE AND A 'CHAIR' IGNORED

I did a deal of teaching, and although centred in Newcastle-upon-Tyne continued to serve on the Panel of Examiners for the General Nursing Council of Scotland.

The examination system is unsatisfactory, but it is difficult to find an appropriate substitute and it seems particularly unsuitable when dealing with nurses, whose function is much more than a knowledge of academic theory or bits and pieces of medical jargon. I am more concerned with the 'suitability' of a girl, and during the viva sessions any cultivated female who impressed me with her personality got off to a flying start. If I felt that I, personally, would have been happy to be nursed by her, she started with a pass of 51% without having opened her mouth and based only upon personality.

I then covered a range of straightforward basic questions, and if she dealt with them adequately she rose to 60%, a useful mark to fuse with that from the written papers, and almost certainly enough to guarantee a pass. I then touched upon a few more difficult topics and if she coped well she rated 75%. In every case, if the girl suffered with poise, and treated me as a civilised person who was not thinking up 'dirty' questions for the sheer joy of failing her she got a further bonus of 5%.

On the other hand, an uptight suspicious girl, badly groomed or with suspect nails and toilet had to fight her way through and do well indeed before she could outstrip her handicap. I had had enough of hatchet-faced sisters in my own earlier days and wished to have no part in launching any more, but the dear ladies of the Nursing Council would have had a fit had they appreciated my attitudes. As it was, we lived contentedly with one another for many years and what they did not know did them no harm.

In Newcastle I also found myself dealing with many final year medical students who were uptight about ordeals ahead and few seemed to remember the old slogan 'PEOPLE DO PASS'. Mostly they felt that there might be a conspiracy to fail them – which was absurd.

That apart, there was no student problem. Students were still respected and Tariq Ali with his fellow leftists had not yet started to foment discontent. The academic life suited me, and I enjoyed teaching. Practical surgery figured less in my programme and I respected, more than ever, the new approach to patients which had been forced upon the medical world by a war. Only decently trained people were now allowed to operate, and surgeons-in-charge saw to it that their juniors were effectively supervised. The surgical free-for-all which I had come to know in Leamington and London had largely disappeared and there was a new sense of responsibility around. Patients, too, were still grateful for advances which seemed miraculous. Penicillin had captured every imagination, and although still painful and usually given by injection, patients appreciated that cures were swift beyond expectation.

Professor Grey-Turner also read my completed monograph and approved. Herbert Bentley equally approved, and everyone was kind when the book was finally accepted by the publisher.

A strange little incident then took place which I can recall in detail. Professor Grey-Turner had taken me into a duty-room and laid on coffee before outlining his plans for my future. First, he said, I would be 'organised into' a newish Chair in one of the colonies. It might be Nigeria, and it was certainly likely to be somewhere in Africa. Thereafter, if I so desired, I would, and if all things were equal (which meant if my work was satisfactory) be able to 'land' a chair within one of the lesser universities in Britain. More were being founded every year or so, and there would be no problem about promoting me back to U.K., after which I would be free to compete for the plums as and when they arose.

It all sounded satisfactory. The travel bug was still active and I had made two or three post-war trips back to Europe, so prospect of a few years in Africa appealed. The Emeritus Professor then left me to cope with a tutorial class of final year people and cover a brief operating session. I was preparing to go home when a certain surgeon arrived to see my own chief, who, it happened, was out of town. The man was a 'fashionable' surgeon in top demand by the more wealthy private patients. We were sipping coffee when sister arrived with a large vase of chrysanthemums. He looked at them curiously. 'These are lovely. Can you grow them in this country?'

I explained that a man had not lived until he had done so: told him how to rear stock, prepare soil and disbud to ensure large blooms. He was fascinated and touched the bronze flowers again and again, caressing them with his palms. 'So fleshy! And you say you grow them yourself.' He paused for a long, long, time. 'You know, Mair,' he said at last, 'this makes me feel terribly ignorant. Maybe I've missed too much in life by being the complete professional in one thing only. Don't make the same mistake.'

I knew, in that moment, that Africa and the 'lesser chair' had ceased to matter. Life had more to offer than total absorption in surgery; or medicine; or anything at all, and I remembered old George Henry Edington's advice. It was more important to become a 'whole man' and to strive towards wisdom. A big-shot surgeon who had missed out on chrysanthemums was a poor soul indeed. Where were his priorities?

That night I talked it over with Trudie, who had returned from her stretch with the Save the Children Fund, and I tried to recall everything I had learned since going to Aberdeen four or more years earlier.

I had learned to teach.

I had learned to operate with a reasonable margin of safety to my patients.

I had become a moderately competent diagnostician.

I had published around eleven scientific articles in various medical periodicals in two continents and I had written a book suggesting a small surgical advance.

But what else? What sort of 'other' pictures flashed through my mind?

Days when an Aberdeen chief had taken me out shooting and I had deliberately missed every bird raised on a costly moor!

I had climbed every mountain bar one in Skye and collected at least fifteen Monroes on the Mainland.

The theatre had given us a wonderful spectrum of entertainments.

I had written a little poetry and begun to value words. The trouble was that there were few poets. Many rhymsters or many bards or minstrels of a sort, yes, but few poets. I felt that I wanted to learn more about the source of 'inspiration' and instinct told me that a path towards Wisdom *might* be discovered through the senses of poetry.

Memory also gave me flashes of favourite books, but I saw only enormous gaps in my reading. The gaps, my picture suggested, would fill more than my life. I also saw far horizons: brown girls sitting below palm trees beside the Pacific; strange men still hunting heads in Papua; a flash of the Taj Mahal and visions of starkly blue mosques in Persia. I felt a weird call to cover the world and delve into remote places, and the thought made me relax into a mood of deep contentment when I realised that I still had dreams.

Our future seemed clear. We would return to the Glasgow-Edinburgh area, find a job which would enable us to travel, launch a family at long last, write a book, and, if Fate was kind, eventually cover the world. I would also paint, write, become a father and seek wisdom. Trudie would at last have children, cherish her dogs and grow her flowers. Jointly we would visit strange places, add to our collection of 'antiques', foster a few friendships and try to learn about everything and anything, even if becoming experts in nothing.

When I again met a contact from Saint Andrew's House and was offered a post at Law Hospital, Carluke, Lanarkshire I accepted, though I also remembered Douglas MacAlman's advice and knew that I must soon make a final break. I detested my craft and loathed the act of cutting, but a curious circumstance had made it particularly difficult for me to quit surgery. The practice which I remembered as a child in Troon had become vacant and I had thought that my mother, in particular, would have been keen enough to see a son take over the show which had once been run by her favourite quack, Doctor Roxburgh, the military-looking gentleman in frock coat. The suggestion was rejected out of hand. Even discussion of the pros and cons became impossible. I was already in disgrace for opting out of academic life and it was more than my parents could stomach to see me 'lower myself' into general practice.

It was, of course, perfectly possible for me to have taken my father's oft repeated advice and told him to go to hell. Hadn't he always said that 'no man could be happy unless in a position to tell anyone to go to hell without worrying about the consequences'?

My problem was that the 'consequences' would have worried me. Indeed, I accepted that guilt complexes would make my emotional life intolerable if I insisted the right to shape my own future. Trudie supported my decision. After all, as she so often told me, they were 'nice' people and they 'meant well'. She agreed, however, that for myself they had paved a road to a private hell with their own good intentions. So we talked it over and decided to try and make a go of a seven year stretch, though remembering that if nightmares about popping arteries or scalpels slipping returned in full flower to cause tension, then, parents or no parents, we would go our own way, and they would have to accept the rough after a good deal of smooth. Forty would be the final deadline whether they liked it or not; and it would be necessary to condition them into accepting the idea. It was pure coincidence that the mystical figure 7 seemed to be the number of years separating me from my fortieth birthday. I hoped it would bring me luck.

10 THOU SHALT NOT CRITICISE THE ESTABLISHMENT

Law Hospital was originally built to cover Emergency Medical Service requirements. It sprawled over an expanse of bleak moor and had been sited safe from air-raids. The buildings had also undergone that peculiar series of changes known as semi-permanisation, and, when I arrived, were being modified to cover civilian requirements within a large industrial and rural area.

Joe Bryant, nephew of Sir Arthur, and brother of Ben Bryant V.C., was consultant physician. The superintendent, Doctor Smart, was a curious hang-over from other days who still tried to run our show like a military operation. He also had a deep and ingrained respect for Authority. John Park of Strathaven was his deputy, a decent, big man with a bluff manner and long experience in general practice. The surgeon whom I was – or so I was told – intended to replace, was a Mr Wenger whose family had interests in the Potteries, and who was anxious to leave surgery in order to join the firm. James Garden was orthopaedist and there was also an anaesthetist and an assorted mixture of 'other ranks' as the superintendent called them.

There was also a matron, and she was in dispute with her staff! I arrived at exactly the wrong time. After various efforts to correct grievances the nursing staff had finally organised a 'round robin' signed by most, if not all, the sisters and nurses. Four senior medical staff also signed. As fifth arrival I was invited to add my own signature and make the thing unanimous. I listened to the story, was sympathetic, and signed on the dotted line.

Law Hospital came under the administrative control of a new organisation called the Western Region Hospital Board whose adviser was a certain Doctor Bowman, and I rated Bowman as a personal friend. The whole set-up, of course, was controlled by faceless individuals operating from Saint Andrew's House, Edinburgh, and it was Saint Andrew's House, Edinburgh,

125

which took control when our complaint arrived a few days later. It was interpreted as a criticism of the Matron, which, after all, it was intended to be. I was surprised only that this was taken a stage further. Criticism of the Matron seemingly implied criticism of those who had appointed her, and the people who had done so drank coffee in Saint Andrew's House! So I had, in real fact, together with four other medical colleagues and the whole nursing staff, challenged the might of Scotland's top Organisation.

It became clear, right from the beginning, that there would be no safety in numbers and that we had much to learn. I first realised that trouble had broken when I was actually summoned from my operating theatre to attend a meeting in the superintendent's office. I was scrubbed up; the patient was prepared for anaesthesia; the theatre was ready for action. Even so, the fish-cold official who had descended from Edinburgh insisted on my presence and seemed disinterested either in inconvenience caused to others (including my patient) or stress induced in the patient through delay.

The atmosphere within Smart's office was arctic and explanations as to our 'disloyal conduct' were demanded. We were allowed no defence but found guilty of 'disloyalty to our superiors', 'of promoting disloyalty among the nursing staff, to whom our conduct ought to have been an example' and of 'inaccuracy in our accusations bearing upon the Matron'. The word 'superiors' especially appealed to me!

Since we had not been allowed, and never were allowed to put forward our case, the meeting was a waste of time, so I returned to my patient and the senior medical staff involved got together later that day in my own home. I had already contacted the Senior Adviser to the Western Regional Hospital Board, my old friend Bowman, and been able to gather from the way in which he stalled every question that no help would be coming from that quarter. On the contrary, I got a shrewd idea as to what might eventually really happen, and so it proved.

John Park, as Deputy Superintendent, was to be transferred to another hospital. Mr Wenger, who had expected to be released from the Emergency Medical Service to enter his family business (where he was urgently needed owing to various private circumstances), was directed, instead, to the army. Jim Garden was also to be disciplined, though I forget exactly how. Joe Bryant was ordered north to a posting far from his liking and I was slightly more sympathetically treated because, apparently, the Organisation accepted that I had been caught up by the tide of events and had signed only to make complaints unanimous.

Such transfers, of course, take time, and it is not practical to remove men from an appointment on twenty-four hours' notice. So we used the time to contact our Member of Parliament, through whom we were able, eventually, to deal with the Secretary of State for Scotland. Sentences were then commuted and and transfers for all but Bryant were cancelled, though Joe did agree to point north, allegedly to fill a temporary appointment as locum, after which he would either return to Law or be given the permanent appointment.

This Bryant situation eventually became fascinating. The vacancy for which he was serving as locum was due to be advertised, and Joe had every reason to believe that he would be given the post, a development which would have been much to his liking. It so happened, however, that Bowman let it slip during conversation with myself that the Organisation intended to advertise the appointment with an age limit of forty-five, and that the advert would not be put out until *after* Joe's forty-fifth birthday – a piece of career assassination of which I disapproved. I also discovered that the Department then intended to send Joe to an alternative post which would not please him.

Armed with this news further meetings were convened in my own home and our Member was once again involved. The end point was that Joe eventually did return to Law Junction Hospital as senior physician. This time, however, I myself paid the full price. Greater love hath no man, than . . . !

The original promise had been that I should succeed Mr Wenger as surgeon-in-charge. Allan MacFarlane had arrived as a junior. Allan was not only well trained but a singularly attractive and competent person, and it had begun to look as though my unit was building up when, out of the blue, a certain Mr Brandon sauntered in to take charge as senior while I was given a very different status, a curious title which was awarded to persons rated insufficiently experienced to merit consultant rank.

So I became Senior Hospital Medical Officer and learned, yet again, how the Organisation copes with rebels and how 'disloyalty' is the ultimate sin.

I decided, however, to play everything cool and to be as gentlemanly as possible about the whole affair. After all, the prophet Job also had problems. There seemed to be no point in becoming involved in conflict with Brandon so we gave him our house to live in, while we were abroad on a four week tour of Central Europe, to enable him to find quarters, feeling that this, at least, would prove how I had no intention to invite conflict.

Brandon, however, was an interesting study. He had been, for some years, a general practitioner, and I was amused when I later heard rumours that he considered I had not been properly trained. He was dead-pan, withdrawn, reserved and smoked a pipe. One story lifts a corner of the Brandon curtain: Allan MacFarlane had been praising what he had seen of certain flower-beds around the Brandon house but was told in my presence, that if he, Brandon, had his way they would be lifted and the beds covered with either asphalt or cement. This seemed to myself to sum the man up. We found nothing in common – and I never saw him operate. I doubt if, in eight years we had a total of eight hours' conversation. Personally, I seldom saw him laugh. My own promotion to consultant came through in due course (very due course), but was of little importance. Long-term plans had been laid between my brother and myself to work together in general practice when and where it seemed to be appropriate. Law was to be my last lap in surgery, and a situation out of which I proposed to extract as much leisure as possible to deal with other matters which seemed more important. My 'grade' simply did not matter, except financially, and that did not matter terribly much either. Brandon mattered even less – and the organisation not at all.

I rated myself as one of the last real 'general surgeons'. I had been trained by very great men, had opened heads and chests, dealt with thoracoplasties and a certain amount of peripheral nerve work. I had covered the field of abdominal surgery and handled much orthopaedics. The ear, nose and throat field had become familiar so far back as Leamington, and I had even developed a special interest in the rarified problems of tendon repair. Gynaecology had been my familiar until leaving Aberdeen and I was not afraid to accept obstetric emergencies. I had solid experience of laboratory techniques, and my researches had been well received.

The war, however, and very fortunately, had changed everything. 'General surgeons' now carried out only a limited number of procedures within the abdomen and few elsewhere, if one excepts varicose veins and removal of the female breast (mastectomy). Brandon seemed suited to be a post-war general surgeon. Orthopaedic surgeons were annually increasing the scope of their own new field, while peripheral nerve units, plastic centres, neuro-surgery departments and the like neatly carved the whole operating area into several specialities, each as important as the other.

Together with this, a gulf was beginning to yawn between teaching centres and peripheral non-teaching hospitals. Students were being angled away from the periphery and somehow being made to feel that good work equated only with teaching units. I also found, among the new generation of younger surgeons which had been thrown up by the war, only few cultivated men who could inspire students as did the giants who had taught in Edinburgh, Glasgow, Aberdeen or London a few years earlier. There was a change in atmosphere which seemed to me unfortunate at best and sinister at worst. If I was right in my judgement, the future would see hosts of limited specialists, each expert in a few technical procedures but with little of the humanity or warmth which had characterised most of their own teachers.

Brandon encouraged an occasional short session with juniors in which one of them would read some sort of 'paper' and then deal with questions. In other days, a senior had directed conversation along fascinating lines of reminiscence, history, philosophy and broad-spectrum gossip which, in the long-run, became more important than, for example, discussion about a new American method of removing the prostate gland or the opinion of a German physiologist about prolonging life through freezing processes. But, of course, Brandon was a different sort of person and I imagine he was happier listening rather than in contributing. Yet I had to admit that the public would benefit from all the changes. Lives were likely, everywhere, to be a much better risk than they had been in English provincial hospitals a few years earlier – and I regretted only that this would be due, not to increased skills of big men, but to little men using advances made freely available by a few research workers, even if using them by rule of thumb. The public would certainly benefit, but I doubted if doctors would ever again be quite the same sorts of people that they had been before.

One remarkable administrative decision which was early built in to the National Health Service promoted much resentment. So-called Merit Awards were, and are, a strange phenomenon. Andrew Muir, now senior physician at Law Junction Hospital, is interesting because he is the only man I know who quite certainly possesses a 'Merit Award'. Curiously enough, modern medicine is the only profession where a man is not supposed to tell even his best friend that he has been granted one, and since this book of 'confessions' discusses various odd situations the merit award absurdity cannot be ignored. It seems to be a device intended to boost selected salaries, and there are three grades. 'A' is substantial and runs well into four figures. 'B' is still very substantial while 'C' is a sort of sop to the pride of those who receive it. Specialists (*sic*) apply for Merit Awards, and as one said quite recently, 'the idea is that one applies annually to explain why one is more meritorious than one was a year earlier'. When granted there seems to be a ban on admitting the fact and few men are willing to discuss it: not at least, until they retire. So, presumably, considerable pressure is brought to bear in order to guarantee secrecy.

It is rumoured that around one third of consultants receive one, but few believe that many are issued outside teaching hospitals, and since Law Junction Hospital is not a teaching centre it follows that Andrew Muir's Merit Award has captured imagination. He is respected on all counts but clearly he is also an individualist and not afraid to say that he has been given one. Which is a small defiance which is somehow important. The merit award situation offends. I cannot begin to understand what rationale lies behind the system, but one thing seems reasonably certain: Government by its tactics, is promoting the suggestion that there is less 'merit' within peripheral hospitals than in teaching centres.

This is so because it is generally assumed (and it can *only* be assumed, since people involved do not seem willing to talk) that individuals in charge of teaching units each have, *ex officio*, at least a Grade 'C' award, and that occupants of chairs are given a Grade 'A'. If so, the assumptions involved are preposterous. I recall Sir Robert Muir's prediction that I would live to see the 'yes-men bum-suckers' take over, and in some cases this has been true. There are certain hospitals where men come to mind who demonstrate the sheerest mediocrity in terms of competence, character and achievement, while there are other more outlandish units, such as Law, where men of great capacity serve without central recognition. I have already lived long enough to realise that Sir Robert's predictions have been fulfilled. 'Yes-men' are now more to be desired by all administrations than individualists, and few administrations go along with free-thinkers, even if their free-thinking leads to recognition in other places.

A more recent example of parochial attitudes and narrow horizons comes to mind in the case of Doctor Hugh Simpson, presently of Glasgow Royal Infirmary. He is a *really* important international personality because of his own original work bearing upon causes of dysrhythmia and stress phenomena in general. He is one of the most cultivated professional men in Scotland today, and among the top in Britain. Yet, for long he had little assistance, by comparison with what was required, and what he was entitled to expect, from Glasgow University, even if he was assisted by the Medical Research Council and fortified by all manner of offers from the United States of America. He rates 'A plus' as a research physiologist, as a research pathologist, as an explorer and holder of the Polar and Mungo Park medals, as photographer, lecturer, editor and scholar. Specifically, his research in chrono-biology – perhaps the baby of modern medical science – may contribute towards introducing a new era in therapeutics and break-throughs in the treatment of malignancy. A Nobel prize during the 80s would in no way surprise me, yet he had to face years of struggle within his own area, and funds were often available only from his own pocket or through the loyal help of his wife, Myrtle, whose earnings as author and international lecturer contributed without reservation towards costly field work and experiment.

The whole question of medical professional earnings also became important at Law. When the National Health Service was launched, salary scales for doctors were unjustifiably low but they are now (1974) in my view, too high and I doubt if they can be justified. However, a pattern has been established and salary adjustments (pay claims, so to speak) are made at more or less irregular intervals, though the old gulf remains between hospital staff at top level (especially bearing in mind the merit award situation) and family doctors. It is arguable that they are all too high. Adjustment should be made only to bring family doctors into line with hospital scales. Senior family doctors should also be graded as specialists in General Practice, and put on the same salary scale as hospital staff.

Way back in the later forties we watched the N.H.S. suffer its abour pains from Law Junction Hospital and few of us were enchanted. Little did we imagine that the birth would produce such a perversely uncontrollable monster!

Few things are more fascinating than the workings of a human mind and Law was, perhaps, interesting in that we provided virtually no psychiatric care. It seems that this became annually more important only after the Welfare State had been launched and when 'total security' had begun to play havoc with people's emotions. Coincidentally there began to be launched that non-stop series of tranquillisers, anti-depressants and stimulants which now seem essential to every 'advanced' country forced to accept 'progress'. During the early 1950s, however, the situation was quite different. Those many family doctors with whom, and for whom I worked in Law seldom referred to patients suffering from stress diseases, yet nowadays it is difficult to meet a doctor who is not ready to talk off the cuff for hours about people who are hooked on one or other of the still respectable drugs.

From this angle the 1940s also seem to have been in another world. Not even during the heat of our early confrontation with Saint Andrew's House did any of us, so far as I know, ever think about taking any sort of drug at all: not even a harmless sleeping capsule. Twenty-five years later it has become standard for persons exposed to purely minor stress to demand 'something for their nerves'. Mental attitudes of patients and doctors alike have changed more than new generations imagine. Self-reliance has faded with self-discipline.

Hospital work had become stereotyped. However, several years earlier, and after a dance in Glasgow, relief came for myself when Jim Galloway once unexpectedly suggested 'writing a sort of *San Michele?*' He said it half in fun, but the idea appealed and eighteen months later, in 1949, Heinemann published my first non-medical book: *Surgeon's Saga*. Since my medical ethical committee disapproved of doctors exposing themselves to publicity and since I was then prepared to toe the official ethical line and had not yet learned the extent to which Establishment rules by unfounded fear, I was obliged to use a pseudonym, and I chose Robertson MacDouall – MacDouall having been my Granny's maiden family name and Robertson my mother's. In the event *Surgeon's Saga* was no *San Michele*, but it did end with the central figure starting off as a family doctor, and was a sign-post showing how I intended to angle my life. It sold two editions in hard-back, but the book also revealed a sad little human story when a certain Mrs Daisy Holden from South East London, wrote to ask where I had discovered a poem used in the text. It was short, but appealing.

> Life is a song.
> God writes the words.
> But WE set them to music at leisure.
> And the song is sad
> Or the song is glad
> As WE choose to fashion the measure.

Her second letter explained that she was a god-daughter of Florence Nightingale, that she lived with an elderly and sick husband, that she had no children and was very poor and very lonely. She had written the poem during a children's party, when the hostess had asked each child to 'do' something, and she had made a second copy. She did not know what had happened to the original left behind after the party, but she had never heard of it again or thought much about it until she read my book. Discovery that her poem had survived close upon sixty years and then been published gave her a new lease of life. She was anxious to meet me.

Her request made me feel unexpectedly shy, and in the event we never did meet, but for several years my father looked her up every time he was in London and told me that she was grateful for a twist of fate which had enabled her to contribute, just a very little, to men's thoughts. Since then I have used her lines to wind up scores of luncheon club lectures or after-dinner speeches and feel that I almost have a 'mission' to preserve her work.

Our son, Craig, was born in 1948 and both Trudie and I learned another sharp lesson which nearly ended in tragedy. Bearing in mind my still vivid memories of London, and our belief that it was folly to be a private patient within a private nursing home, we felt that there was still a place for nursing homes involving a simple business like a confinement. But how wrong we were! The consultant who served Trudie went home shortly after the birth and remained out of touch for some days. When I arrived at the Nursing Home staff behaved as though the child was already dead, and I saw our son only after much argument. He had, in fact, a massive plug of mucous deep down in his trachea, was able to breathe only with difficulty and was virtually certain to die unless oxygen was laid on and the plug removed.

There was no oxygen available and matron said it would be impossible to get any before such-and-such a day. She allowed me to use her phone only with strange ill grace and I myself contacted British Oxygen direct. Minutes later a cylinder was being rushed to the home, and, since our consultant was 'unavailable' and no one else had been laid on to stand in for him, Craig Borland and I slipped a tube into the infant's throat, switched on the oxygen and watched his colour improve within seconds. The consultant is being treated with undeserved generosity in that I do not give his distinguished name.

It still remained to get the mucous removed, and it was again unfortunate that the 'only man in Glasgow capable of using a bronchoscope in such a young infant' was out of town, so Craig and I supervised the child almost night and day until, by what seemed a miracle of good fortune he himself coughed the plug up on the third and was finally out of danger.

Never again, I vowed! Never, just never, would I go back upon my resolution. Hospital was the only place in which to be ill, and the only place to have a first baby. It is not surprising that the infant was christened Craig. Craig Borland's services in the nursing home were only the latest in a long series, mostly rendered without realising the fact.

Our second son arrived sixteen months later, and his medical history also became interesting. I give his story in brief only to illustrate a quality of arrogance which has now, I think, lessened. The child developed pneumonia but failed to respond well to antibiotics in full dose, and the condition left him with a collapsed right lower lobe and a persistent lung abscess.

When the collapse was first noted a certain senior paediatrician assured me that the lung would re-expand within days, made an appointment for two weeks later and refused to react when I advised him daily by phone that the lung was not, as predicted, re-expanding. I continued to take the precaution of having a chest X-ray carried out more or less every second day and had proof that the lobe was still collapsed. Even so, the paediatrician refused to see the child again, said that it was the 'old story of a medical family being over-anxious', and insisted that the boy be taken to see him only on the appointed day, still some time ahead.

I did as requested, took Leonard in by car together with the X-rays and watched the man's reaction as he studied them. It was little satisfaction to see him change colour and his fingers begin to tremble. He knew as well as I did that he had failed in his duty, and that I was in a position to make a deal of trouble.

I removed the child without saying anything other than that we wished nothing more to do with him, and motored to Edinburgh where we had an appointment with Andrew Logan. Decision was made that removal of the diseased lobe would be almost inevitable, but Mr Logan suggested we wait for a year to see how matters progressed.

Relapses, bouts of infection, cough and persistent spit were handled by our family doctor, Oliver Grey of Wishaw, who is also one of the giants, and the lobectomy was carried out after over two years of anxiety. During the middle fifties removal of a lung or part of a lung was a different proposition from the standardised procedure which is now accepted as almost commonplace and we were at ease in our minds only because we knew that if Andrew Logan could not save him no one else could. The result, in fact, was so satisfactory that as an adult he is not now even loaded for insurance and lives a normal life.

One part of me still regrets that I did not sue the paediatrician. The capital which no doubt would have been received would have been useful when Leonard set up house, and he would certainly have been given compensation, because the paediatrician's real mistake was in refusing to see the child when requested and having been given important information. His offence was professional negligence and his behaviour was quite unethical, especially when the request came from a responsible colleague. The experience made me sympathetic to all patients who insist upon a second opinion, and very antipathetic towards any consultant who tries to avoid seeing them (which does happen from time to time).

Trudie made the ideal mother, but her thoughts cast far ahead, and a few years later she gave me a small collection of verses which showed me how her mind was working. Some of them so much reflect a little of her personality that they will interest all who know her.

Shoes

My shoes are done – they let in water.
Throw them out – they're just no use.
Let's go shopping, buy some new ones,
Shoes to match my summer suit.

But do we think of all our footwear
And all the stories they can't tell
Of endless pleasures mixed with sorrows?
Our footwear knows them very well.

Little babies in their bootees
Stumble on, until, one day
The first few steps alone are taken.
Bootees proudly show the way.

Then we say – 'Oh look! He's walking.'
It's time he had some stronger shoes.
Farewell bootees – gone for ever –
Now it's leather – hurts your toes.

Leather shoes take him out walking.
Seeing much in life that's new.
But – alas – they're soon disfigured
Kicking stones as boys all do.

Church bells, ringing, call the faithful.
The little chap in feathers fine
Wearing church shoes – bright and shiney –
Is introduced to things Divine.

Shortly after, school approaches –
Bringing thoughts of rain and sleet.
Wellie boots come up from nowhere
Exciting powerful tiny feet.

Then the pace is stepped up quickly.
Gym shoes – football boots and all.
If he's lucky he'll go skating.
Skating boots make boys walk tall.

So time goes on, our lad goes dancing
As generations did before.
He wears the kilt and shoes with buckles
While dancing lassies round the floor.

They're happy shoes, the ones with buckles.
They lead to courtship and romance.
And escort girls with high heels homewards
To fix a date for next week's dance.

Not always is the path so easy.
When escort is refused he's sad.
Again kicks stones in aimless fashion.
Thoughts of 'High-heels' drive him mad.

Then comes Spring. Shoes are suède now.
His step is light. Song fills the air.
He's off – with diamond in his pocket
To conquer 'High-heels' in her lair.

Once more the Church-bells ring out calmly
For a symphony in black and white.
Our boy and girl are now united –
Step out proudly, bathed in Light.

Trudie Mair

Family health apart, everything else prospered. My belief that the days of old-style 'general surgery' were over was confirmed. Law expanded into a solid, useful entity. Staff had risen to the challenge of creating something new and been successful. 'Recent' advances infiltrated into all our lives and patients' expectation of recovery improved. My hernia book actually brought me a patient from India in order to have a post-operative problem dealt with by my whole skin graft technique. The original operation, which led to his rupture, had been carried out in London, and I still find it remarkable that this very careful gentleman, himself a surgeon, chose me to cope with the complication. I refused, as I have almost always done, to treat him as a private patient, other than to lay on an 'amenity room' but he rewarded me generously before flying home.

To round off the story: it is remarkable that he also insisted on my treating a hernia which developed elsewhere several years later, and when I had withdrawn from surgery. His insistence that I do the operation was so great that I reluctantly agreed and made a last come-back, with James Galloway assisting. The skin graft technique was again used and the patient was in good condition years later. I make the point only to underline that satisfaction which a doctor knows when he achieves such a degree of trust in the doctor-patient relationship, a fact which it is possible many patients do not much consider or appreciate.

Meanwhile, in 1953, my brother who had had earlier thoughts of becoming a physician, quit hospital service, and we confirmed earlier plans to organise a family doctor set-up which would enable us both to expand personal interests. Our theory was that if two men ran a one-man practice there would be ample time to do 'other things'.

We eventually selected Grangemouth as our centre of operations. There were opportunities in other places, but Grangemouth had certain attractions. The town was small being not more than one-and-a-half miles square, was flat and an exercise in time and motion. There was also full employment and housing conditions in general were good. There were few real slum areas and we had both become interested in the new social problem which was developing. People, as my brother and I saw it, were becoming morally corrupted by 'security', by 'progress', by swiftly increasing standards of living and by politicians who continually promised MORE.

The Welfare State had been born to a fanfare of verbal trumpets which blasted the new national slogan: 'protection from cradle to the grave'. But *Protection* had been swiftly amended to *Security*, and we sought a human laboratory where we might examine the 'progress situation' at first-hand among people who really were 'secure' and who had more of everything than my Mauchline Hunger Marchers could ever have imagined almost thirty years earlier.

An elderly Doctor Anderson was due to retire. Alistair joined him as assistant with a view to succession, and when the older man had withdrawn I joined my brother. We arranged the hospital holiday allowance of '42 days not counting Sundays', which meant 49 days in practice; and we had an arrangement through which either of us could take virtually unlimited 'extra' time for a realistic fiscal penalty – for daily locum rates, to be precise. Since there were several months to wait before Doctor Anderson wished, finally, to leave I decided to pass the time by making a trip to Japan as ship's surgeon on a cargo passenger boat. The voyage took longer than was expected and I returned several weeks late to take over the 'practice house' and start a new career at 39. Recent dreams had again proved that surgery was not for me.

I was sorry to leave my friends in Law. Yet if Law taught me anything at all it was the way in which the Organisation worked in Edinburgh, and exactly how ruthless it could be when things came to a show-down.

My leisure hours, however, had taught me a great deal, and my Far East trip taught me even more, most of which proved invaluable when I became a family doctor, odd though that suggestion may sound. An odd thought crossed my mind during return from Japan. The paediatrician who had neglected Leonard had really escaped court proceedings because of a dream years earlier when I had awakened to write a poem and vowed to 'let my weapons be', amongst other things, 'charity' and 'kindness'. On the face of everything this seemed rather absurd, but it also underlined the importance which I still attached to an experience which could not be explained.

Life, it seemed, could be influenced by major decisions motivated by small experiences. I had rejected a chair of surgery because a senior consultant knew nothing about chrysanthemums. I had been merciful to a negligent physician because of a young man's dream. I had met my wife because of a casual meeting with a nurse. I had begun to respect my parents because of Trudie's compassion. I had originally begun to believe in life on another dimension because, as a child, I had seen a fairy which others said must have been a butterfly. I had sacrificed some years of income and seniority at Law because of sheer chance compelling me to be loyal to men who were, at the time, complete strangers. I had rejected wealth and an adoptive mother because of a compulsion to resist her bullying of junior nurses.

Already, by the later thirties I had begun to accept a curious sense of predestination and the conviction that I would be allowed to live for so long as I justified the confidence of a goddess with whom I seemed to be in periodic communication. It was all very reassuring, even if dreams had so plagued my life as a surgeon that I was now totally repelled by the sight of knives or blood.

I even understood that Trudie's incredible compassion and loyalty were changing me deep down inside, and when I remembered again our first meeting, and the certainty which I had felt that we would marry, I knew, just knew, without reservation, that my tiny life was part of a greater plan and that, preposterous though it might seem, I did mean something to people who mattered.

11 TRAVEL POT-POURRI

Never, throughout the years, had I lost sight of the need to waste time sensibly and the Japanese escapade was a roaring success which provided a first travel book. My publisher felt that any title using the word 'doctor' would sell, and *Doctor Goes East* did not do so badly.

Highlights during the trip were sometimes almost sensational, but possibly because there were virtually no passengers I got to know most ports backwards because an excellent relationship with skipper and officers allowed me to leave the ship for days on end. Trudie claimed, when I returned, that I had changed. She still says that I 'was never the same again', and I don't argue, because it was the first time in my life when I had really been able to find my own level in worlds as far removed from my own as anything on this globe can reasonably be, and at every port I had travelled many miles from the ship to visit unusual people many of whom were less than socially acceptable in terms of my tribal norms.

So how could I argue that I had not changed?

How could I then realise that the whole 'time-wasting' experience would be invaluable when dealing with Grangemouth? Instinct, however, told me that I had done the right thing. Conversations way back in the old days had underlined the importance of broad-spectrum involvement with life, but the curious thing was that the more I learned the less I seemed to understand. I was less dogmatic about asserting opinions and more interested in listening to other points of view. Truth, I had begun to discover, was an elusive creature and true wisdom rare as a truly happy man.

Alistair was relieved when our firm finally got off the ground. Patients were curious to inspect the new doctors, and work boomed.

When a principal retired, while it was *expected* that his flock would 'be faithful to a door' and join the new man, they were officially notified of their legal right to change and given several months to make up their minds. It seemed that they were going to vet us in detail before reaching any decision. There was also another reason for our heavy work load. Our predecessor had left us neither case records nor reports from consultants, so every patient had to be examined very thoroughly to establish a base line – and this took time. Since we had decided to keep records similar to those we used in hospital, note-taking was also time-consuming. Yet patients sat, without complaint and sometimes for a couple of hours before being seen, but knowing that when they were they would be given a detailed overhaul. So a pattern was established! Most of our 3,000 people must have arrived within the next few months and all were given an assessment which proved that we had a deal of spring-cleaning ahead.

Since we had also decided to start as we meant to continue we did not allow any patient to choose either one of us to be *his* doctor, but because we filed full notes covering every visit people swiftly appreciated that it did not matter which of us they did attend. They began in fact, to realise that there was continuous benefit from two opinions, and, so far as we could judge, they seemed to like it. Our show was really run along the lines of an out-patient clinic in hospital, and since there was no 'appointments system' each person was seen for as long as might be necessary, often for upwards of twenty minutes or more. Our methods depended partly upon keeping our case records comprehensive.

Right from the beginning the question obviously arose as to how many people could be efficiently handled along these lines, and it was our belief that the 'lines' were almost ideal. We even financed a secretary-receptionist out of our meagre earnings, but since we had to live, we wanted to boost our list to a more financially realistic level, though we were not prepared to increase it beyond a figure which we felt equated with the chance of giving quality service. We therefore launched field research to discover exactly how many patients a man could properly handle. The empirically decided legal maximum allowed was originally 4,000, but we felt that it was much too high and wished to establish guide lines to a more ideal level. Our findings, published in the *British Medical Journal* (*Brit. Med. Jour. 2.* Suppl. p. 281) after a five year study suggested that 2,000 was the ceiling, but in order to offer a figure more acceptable to politicians we finally settled for 2,500. In the event, Dr Richard Scott of Edinburgh's Faculty of General Practice told me privately that, in his view, 1,500 was the really ideal maximum. So, on the Scott assessment, Alistair and I were exactly right with a combined list of 3,000, though in terms of salary it was ludicrous.

We were also able to satisfy ourselves that the basic premises upon which remuneration of family doctors were based within the National Health Service were not compatible with good work. It therefore became important *not to lose patients*. With a joint list of less than 3,000 we would be almost bankrupt, as we operated on only a small profit margin. This problem came to a head after I had been only a few months in Grangemouth where our next door neighbour was a respected citizen believed to be influential. According to Alistair he was one of a select few who could ruin us if they chose. He was also a patient, and I had been advised to treat him with care.

Events, as have so often been the case in my life, moved swiftly. Trudie and I had fixed to go to Switzerland with the family for a month, and we felt guilty. Even so we still proposed to begin as we meant to continue, though conscience made us slink off at the crack of dawn before the town had come to life. It is just a pity that I forgot how our elderly neighbour daily visited his laundry with the lark!

We met while I was entering our car and he stopped dead to stare at me curiously. 'Where are *you* off to?'

'On leave.' I felt myself flushing.

He narrowed his lips and looked very prim. 'The trouble in this town is that the doctors are aye on leave. They don't think enough about honest work.'

I stepped out of the car, walked to the wall which separated us and asked him a question. 'Why don't you mind your own business you interfering old bastard?'

The incident ruined our holiday, but when we returned I heard that our neighbour had been amused and had admired my 'repartee', after which I felt that anything could happen, and that there really was nothing stranger than folk – a fact which was underlined when a fifteen-year-old girl, who could easily have passed for eighteen, popped into my office one evening to find out whether or not she was pregnant. She was relaxed about her situation, but gave an unexpected reply when I asked how she had got into difficulties.

'I like measuring them,' she said, and opened a horizon which, until then, had been closed even to fantasy. She was obsessed about the comparative size of penises, and padded the docks, visited the pubs or lurked in lanes, armed with an inch tape, condoms and a tube of K.Y. jelly. The more she measured the more she became interested, and she accepted as a matter of course that she had finally to co-operate or males became awkward. She had run out of condoms one evening but been unable to resist speculating about a West African whom she found 'up a close' and thought that 'that was when it might have happened'.

It was then my turn to ask an unorthodox question. 'How had he rated?' She looked sour. 'Seven inches dead.'

Her heftiest to date had been a Cockney deck-hand who reached eight-and-a-half inches, and her smallest 'was a wee chap from India or somewhere' who managed 'only three and a bit'.

The girl was an exception to normal rule. Women are not usually interested in the dimensions of male equipment, and although a popular topic in pornographic books or cartoons the concept is based upon fantasy. It is men who are sensitive, and their fears or self-consciousness are usually based upon notions springing from ignorance of facts plus ideas born from the boastings of others.

144

My fifteen-year-old eventually became an authority on the subject, and since her pregnancy fears proved to be a false alarm she carried on as before, though taking care never to run short of condoms. She married five years later after 'measuring' over six hundred men, and it may interest male readers to know that her average eventually worked out at six-and-one-quarter inches from pubis to top of glans with the apparatus primed for action. Her one 'freak' was a German engineer who touched nine-and-a-quarter inches, and the man of her choice was, she told me during her last visit, exactly six. Since she settled down well and seems to be happily married this should reassure uptight Casanovas who eat oysters or drink raw eggs.

The girl taught me a great deal. More, in fact, than I learned at college, and since I have been able to double-check almost everything through other sources it can do no harm to list her likes and dislikes – which were mostly 'normal' and factual.

Sex photographs or pornographic pictures left her cold: as they do a majority of women.

She discovered that the use of four letter words while lovemaking switched the average man on more quickly than anything else, and she was emphatic that 'the more prim-and-proper they were the more they liked it'.

She said that women had few secrets from one another and gossiped about their sex life freely while men got hang-ups about talking to other men.

She found it easy to organise a triangle of two girls and one man, but difficult to fix using two men and one girl.

She felt that men were peeping toms and women exhibitionists.

She had nothing but contempt for males who practised *coitus interruptus* or were selfish and did not understand 'that women wanted it too'.

She felt that most unplanned pregnancies came to couples who thought 'withdrawal' was safe.

She said that Negroes were not 'any better or bigger' than 'whites' and that women who thought they were would be due for a disappointment.

She was an enthusiast for both fellatio and cunnilingus but

145

only where she knew the men well. She was also sure that fellatio was the second fastest way to 'get a man going if he was tired', and believed that semen was not only a good general tonic but kept the breasts large and firm.

She believed in ringing the changes with position and felt it was up to every girl to find out through practice the best way to get an orgasm.

My involvement seemed to develop quite naturally. I believed, at first, that she was abnormal and I was anxious to help since I remembered my own blood pressure neurosis. But I knew what had caused my problem and I felt that cure would be brought about only if she discovered the origin of her own particular obsession. She was given hours and hours of time throughout the next few years until I finally decided that she was 'normal'. The only difference was that she lived with reality and not fantasy and that she had courage enough to avoid repressing powerful instincts. Apart from sex behaviour she was a conventional girl, held down a reasonable job, fitted well into family life, enjoyed the usual run of small-town peak-moments and looked forward, 'one day' to marriage with Mr Right. She was also willing to listen to 'reasonable advice' and was taught enough to avoid V.D., get picked up by the police or become socially suspect.

She was probably my most important all-time experience as a family doctor and discussed sex so naturally that it eventually became simple even for myself to cover the whole spectrum of sex relationships with anyone of any age without batting an eyelid, a circumstance which was a far cry from Mauchline and the tabus of Kilmarnock or Troon.

A local priest once told me that family doctors and priests are probably the only professional people 'flung in at deep-ends without either knowledge or training', but, he argued, since no young people could ever believe 'at second hand' the extraordinary behaviour patterns of humanity, time had proved that the best approach was to pitch them into trouble right up to the neck and let them learn the hard way.

Fifteen years had passed since I first proved this in Paisley-Barrhead, but I had half forgotten how challenging general practice could be and I had also forgotten that family doctors really *were* flung in at the deep end. No aspect of formal university training equipped them to deal with emotional problems. Few were either capable or willing to become involved with sex situations. Most were as inhibited as their patients and many had equally unhappy or resigned marriages.

I even discovered that the wife of one particular doctor was still a virgin after a dozen or more years. Their tragedy became known to the small circle coping with the wife's minor gynaecological problems and clearly her husband could no more have handled the stresses of married life as presented across a family doctor's desk than he could have skated down a sunbeam. So he protected himself *against* patients by refusing to become involved. Uptight people received standard placebos or mild doses of phenobarbitone and he never even tried to discover underlying basic causes of tension. Though in this he was no different from most.

Since a deal of time is required before patients feel free to confess their difficulties I handled many of these outside office hours, usually during my off-duty, and almost always in my own home, yet results provided more satisfaction than any other aspect of my work. They gave me a smallish handful of loyal friends who were grateful and they also gave me a smaller number who became so hostile that change of doctor was the only possible end-point. This hostility is almost inevitable when trying to unravel certain situations, but if surmounted it is replaced by loyalty, if not by down-right affection, and certainly by a situation about which something can be done to help.

It is understandable that most family doctors avoid rows, and prefer, since they themselves usually have limited experience of anything but standard textbook problems, to play ostrich. It is even more understandable that fear of publicity, or downright personal ignorance of sex at other than conventional level, makes most doctors lean backwards to off-load responsibility for handling patients demanding education in depth. This problem, fortunately, has largely been overcome by more specific and informed publications such as *She, Nova, Forum, Cosmopolitan* and the like, and by various radio or T.V. plays and features.

During the later '50s I was asked to read a paper at a Stirlingshire British Medical Association meeting. Since I had become interested in society's hypocritical attitudes, and the profession's ostrich-like attitudes to sex, I decided to be provocative and delivered a message which covered the situation as I saw it, but ended by suggesting need for the state to organise brothels in every town with a population of 50,000 or over. I also suggested that these might be made the responsibility of local medical officers of health, and emphasised need for state control to avoid private exploitation.

The paper was a semi-jest and an exploratory 'feeler' to test medical opinion, but I was amazed when the meeting agreed and not one single voice was raised in criticism. A lady doctor even ventured an amendment suggesting that there should be 'facilities for women', an example of practical, but advanced thinking, which hadn't crossed my own more limited imagination. The medical officers of health present spoke amiably about the prospect, and that was that. How matters would have stood had press or public been around is another question, but since we were completely private I imagine that all present were candid and put their views on the line.

The story is important, because it tends to suggest that these men knew very well how much human sorrow is due to sex ignorance or repression, and that in the state brothel concept they saw at least a possible long-term hope for improving the overall situation. I still go along with the idea and realise how much facilities would be used when I think of various patients whose private lives came under my microscope. There was a small handful of executive types, for example, who, when going to London usually contacted an internationally 'known' name in advance and had a selection of call-girls laid on from which they could choose a partner for the weekend at a fifty guinea fee plus routine hotel and board expenses. There was also the larger number of migrant types who commuted around 'sites' at home and abroad, earned big money and spent a proportion of it freely on women, with or without wine and song.

One of our few private patients even ran a fairly costly mistress in a nearby village, and got away with it for a score of years or more. Certain streets also had husband swapping sessions conducted so discreetly that there was no real local gossip, and several good-looking girls from upper-crust families were virtually amateur prostitutes, yet so tight-lipped about their activities that in spite of a fairly extensive clientele in several towns few became locally suspect. One resident manageress in an establishment catering for businessmen provided 'extra' services for any visitor who appealed to her, then contracted gonorrhoea from a distinguished-looking visitor and, oddly enough, after a long separation met him again and married. I even had one stretch of almost two years when around 90% of brides from the firm were in their second month of pregnancy.

Two or three odd cases of incest also came my way, and by and large I concluded that 'they were all at it', or almost all, which, of course, was an exaggeration. Maybe only half of them 'were at it'. But, knowing what I do of small-town sex life in the fifties, official attitudes towards the so-called permissive society of ten years later amused me greatly. One part of the permissive society, for me, has always been a non-hypocritical society, and I imagine that the fifties were a final turning point from post Victorian puritanism, even if sex is still basis for blackmail in areas where it equates with Calvinistic sin concepts. Nor do I believe that Grangemouth was different from most places in Britain. It simply happened that I was licensed to lift the curtain a little, and that patients trusted me enough to confide: often with specific detail.

Given my own chilly upbringing I was personally sensitive about so-called perversions and realised that I had come to cross-roads when asked to give divorce-court evidence on behalf of a patient who wished divorce on grounds of 'unreasonable demands' made by her husband. Her solicitor was astonished when I refused to give evidence and said that not only did I know she enjoyed fellatio sessions with her husband but that I rated this as 'normal'. My opinion was given off the cuff so I must have meant what I said – which was yet one more step forward! I also told him how I knew for a fact, not only that the girl 'liked' fellatio, but that she had taught her husband to perform cunnilingus even before they were married. Understandably my evidence was not thereafter invited.

However, it was one thing to know intimate details about private lives, and another to use them in court – on any pretext.

I had not forgotten months when I had repeatedly broken the Hippocratic oath in England, so I did my best to avoid circumstances in which I might be forced to reveal secrets to an audience wider than a small hospital board, and by and large I did succeed as I wriggled through several cross-examinations without letting patients down. But I disliked the ordeal, and would have gone far to avoid it.

People, however, kept doing the craziest things. One young woman inherited ten thousand pounds from her father together with his house and contents, became engaged shortly afterwards, and was persuaded to sign over everything to her husband, 'to show how much she loved him'. Within two or three years he had moved his mother into the home and thrown his wife out. She became a nervous wreck and was such a pitiable object that my evidence became ruthless. The man was a swine and I fought to the limit to bring his wife as big a settlement as possible.

I especially disliked police work, and loathed being involved in checking patients for alleged drunkenness, believing that there should be a full-time police surgeon of such impartiality that there would be no need to involve the family doctor, who must, by the nature of things be theoretically biased.

The validity of the 80 milligram blood level for alcohol was also debatable and I was glad to co-operate in an experiment in Edinburgh organised by John Blackwood, then editor of the Scottish *Daily Mail* but involving also Edinburgh City Police and the Senior Driving Instructor for Scotland. Two journalists known to be mild to moderate 'social drinkers' were guinea-pigs for our experiment which was carried out in the yards of a major bus depot. The journalists were asked to eat a normal breakfast and to check in at 9.00 a.m. when the police superintendent assesssed them, and the driving instructor took them over a specially prepared course flanked by plastic cones and established an average figure for the number of cones knocked down. It was claimed that results could not be improved by practice and that significant problems of judgement were involved. I then gave them a medical check, recorded blood pressure and pulse, withdrew both urine and blood samples for alcohol assessment and laid on typescript to duplicate in order to decide their average number of errors per page.

They were then given drinks prepared in private by John Blackwood and an impartial observer. Tests were repeated every half-hour, and they drank systematically all day, pausing only for a three-course lunch with coffee. Seven hours after the experiment began the police were unable to fault either man, and the driving instructor was also thwarted. They were going round his courses like experts and seldom even touching a cone. From my own angle, speech and all other clinical tests were also satisfactory and there were fewer-than-at-first typing errors. They even toed white lines, said *truly rural* or *west register street* and *she sells sea shells on the sea shore* without turning a hair.

We broke up in the evening after a series of final tests including blood and urine. Days later the laboratory findings came back with results which were expected, but still remarkable. With alcohol levels far in excess of 250 milligrams per cent (legal upper permissible limit being only 80), it had been impossible for police, doctor or driving instructor to fault the men. Not unnaturally the editor decided that 'it would be against the national interest' to publish our findings, and so far as I know this is the first time they have been made public.

A few years later, one of the test journalists interviewed me for his column and recalled what an effort it had been to 'jack himself up'. Even so, he had managed and, if he could, so could others. Personally I found the results disturbing. It is not possible to lay down the law about how people will react to alcohol. There are too many imponderables. Bearing in mind figures for road accidents, it would be more sensible to ban all 'drink and driving' entirely and to penalise every driver found to have any alcohol whatsoever in his system, as is done in Finland. The figure 80 is a British-type compromise and difficult to justify.

One other eternally vexed question bothered Alistair and myself right from the beginning when we were first confronted with the need to use morphia in unorthodox doses. It had first come to my own attention as a student, when required during an examination in *Materia Medica*, to describe the effects of one half grain (30 milligrams) of morphine sulphate in an adult subject. Most of the candidates wrongly listed an over-dose response, since the standard British Pharmacopoeia figure was then maximum one quarter grain (15 milligrams). In fact, until 1932 or thereabouts the half grain dose was standard and experience of this trick examination question made me alert to the fact that there was more to morphia than met the eye.

I learned literally nothing more in hospital, but proof came dramatically in the case of a middle-aged man with severe coronary artery disease who failed to respond to dosage of one half grain (30 milligrams) given during his first attack in Grangemouth. After hospital treatment lasting over a period of weeks he was referred home to die, an event which did not take place until over a year later, by which time several facts had been established. His pains, which were frequent, responded only to morphine in large dose and the consultant called in to comment upon this advised that we continue to use it. Dose was originally increased only after discussion between two or more people and after everyone was satisfied that there was no alternative. It was also begun *knowing* that dose might well have to be further increased owing to the remarkable tolerance which people may acquire to morphia and its derivatives.

After some months we notified the Medical Practices Committee of the situation. Since the patient was having around twenty grains per day (1,200 mgms) this was necessary in the interests of self-preservation, especially since a doctor in the south of England was then being tried for the murder of several patients whose bodies had been found to contain less than we were using upon a man who seemed to thrive on the stuff. We had also decided that medical evidence led for the Crown in this case was completely uninformed and we had decided that if the doctor was found guilty of either murder or manslaughter we would contact his solicitors and offer to give evidence during appeal. Regarding the murder case, however, the doctor had inherited various gifts of value, a fact which was impossible at our end, but we still felt that he might have been a victim of circumstance.

Our own man finally died after reaching a tolerance of around thirty or more grains (1,800 mgms) of morphine per twenty-four hours. His personality was not debased by the drug. He was kept 'comfortable' only, and repeat only, by that drug, and he was mentally alert right to the end. He was not converted into a drug addict. In fact, and this is very important indeed, he had no morphine whatsoever during his last ten days, and he showed neither withdrawal symptoms nor need for any. This fact may not impress lay readers, but it is of extreme medical significance, because there was a man who should – if all loose talk was accurate, or if most teaching is accurate – not only have been an addicted person, but victim to the most frightful withdrawal ordeals when not given a drug which had been used in such massive doses for over one year. Yet it was not so. His last ten days were pain free he was mentally alert and he was not only happy, but optimistic about his future.

An exception does not prove any rule, but the case of this man provides food for much thought and made us drastically reappraise attitudes to several other drugs including, of course, further study of morphine. Thereafter we quizzed every possible colleague about dose used and effects caused, just as we quizzed every patient known to have been given morphine in hospital, say as a preliminary to anaesthesia. We ended, convinced that the dose was usually inadequate, that the drug was unreasonably feared and misunderstood by most doctors, and that only suggestible patients who knew what they were being given did show any significant response to one quarter grain, and that chiefly because they *expected* to feel sleepy. It was this element of suggestibility which remained much in our minds and which, we finally concluded, did more harm than anything else when the so-called drug-scene of the permissive society broke out some years later.

During my experience in both hospital and general practice I never discovered one single patient who was a drug addict in the popular sense of the word. Though I am ignoring very many 'normal' people who would have screamed with rage had I accused them of being addicts, which they were, one and all, since they were dependent upon one thing or another: but chiefly barbiturates or drinamyl.

I did find, however, a goodly number of panic-stricken mothers who claimed that a son or daughter was 'on drugs' because they were friendly with some teenager who was also 'known' to be 'on drugs'. In no case was there justification for the fear, and the episodes always ended with a bewildered young person wondering why parents had gone crazy and shown no trust. In no case did my follow-up of suspect contacts show one scintilla of evidence to justify rumour. The drug scare was blown up almost beyond belief by panicky parents, gossipy neighbours, exaggeration of minor incidents and much angled publicity through news media.

It seemed plainly foolish, for example, to allow an allegedly responsible person to say, in effect, on radio or television, 'after two years on LSD addicts promote themselves to heroin. It is inevitable'. I could just see, but see, poor little inadequate people who had taken the odd shot of LSD over a two year period reach for their wallet and dive for the black-market knowing that there must be something wrong. After two years they were not on heroin yet! Christ they must be bad! Where is the real hard stuff?

It was even more worrying to hear people go on, and on, and on, saying, in effect: 'all hash addicts finally promote themselves to LSD and the hard drugs'. It was, apart from anything else, not true. But even more important, it was being repeatedly said to an audience including people really inadequate in pure culture, some of whom might very well be on hash, but who because of their basic suggestibility might afterwards 'promote themselves to LSD'. I detest censorship, but I did conclude, and still believe, that there is a case for refusing people freedom to talk *ad lib* about drugs of any kind, and to insist upon a script which has been vetted by really knowledgeable authorities with practice in the field. The media have a deal to answer for in over-stating the drug scene, quite apart from actually 'suggesting' people into risk of expanding it.

Small town gossip has at least as much to be ashamed of, since one single drug episode in a community can be blown out of perspective to an extent which is unbelievable, as was the case locally when a certain school was found to have four or five pupils on soft drugs. After a week or two, most over-anxious mothers in my firm were convinced that their own brood were irredeemably hooked on sinister needles or mind blowing cigarettes and were asking me to cope. It was all very sad, and so unnecessary.

There are, of course, drug addicts just as there are alcoholics, exhibitionists, sado-masochs, muggers and a host of other anti-social people with built-in defects of one sort or another, and I have met drug addicts of every type from Calcutta through Nepal, back to Siam and on into Malaysia, Hong Kong and Japan. What is more, there always have been drug addicts of one sort or another over most of Asia and parts of Afro-Europe. The proportion of soft drugs addicts capable of harming either themselves or society in Western Europe is small and the proportion of tragic people addicted to hard drugs is even less. One and all, however, and within my experience as a world traveller, have been more than usually 'suggestible' and I argue only in favour of avoiding *all* comment which might tend to influence their behaviour.

The drug scene in South East Asia is a very different matter, sprung from very different origins, and posed especially sinister problems within a civil war situation. It bears upon the British scene only in so far as it is given publicity, presented as a defiance of society, or when excused by liberal self-styled intellectuals who may well do more harm than good when given freedom on radio or television to speak 'off the cuff'.

The drug scene is one which, I am very certain, would best respond to a ban on all publicity. It is especially dangerous when ustified as a rebellion by younger people against an effete society.

13   BATTLES IN BOOM TOWN

My own position in Grangemouth was, from the beginning, a little unusual, but unorthodox opinions and willingness to become deeply involved in patients' lives made it more so.

Surgeon's Saga and *Doctor Goes East* had tickled local imagination and many found it odd to have a doctor who was an author, while a television confrontation concerning management of patients in hospital out-patient departments also brought mild local fame, or possibly even notoriety. My opponent on the programme was my (by then) *bête noir*, Doctor Bowman, former adviser to the Western Regional Hospital Board, but now able to 'speak' because he had retired. It was, for myself, an interesting experience to argue through the goggle box points which I felt ought to be publicised. I was both amused and irritated to discover during the next week that no one remembered a single comment made during the whole discussion. In spite of that everyone said that I had 'been great'. I was later to learn that nothing I ever said – right up to the present day – was ever remembered by any viewer who came my way. The opinion that I had been 'great' was not shared by the local Medical Practices Committee.

I was gently advised, behind the scenes, not to get so much publicity, and quietly rebuked for having allowed *Doctor Goes East* to be published under my own name. The arrival of *Doctor Goes North* plus *Doctor Goes West* did nothing to reassure one or two seniors who would not excuse me for having again used my own name. Why, I was asked, could not I have done what Gordon did and used a pseudonym?

Nor was the medical Organisation reassured when my brother published his own first books and *Rue with a Difference* followed by *The Man Within* reached our local library under his own name.

Doctor Goes West had an odd content in that it described my effort to unravel the fate of Colonel Fawcett who had, long earlier, disappeared with two others into Brazil's Matto Grosso. The story involved meetings with strange people, and especially with Miss Universe, Teresinha de Morange, former Miss Brazil, ending with a spectacular gala performance in her honour at Amazonia's once notorious Opera House in Manáos.

A first 'travel lecture' had been launched in 1949 when Spain was still a far-away, unknown place, and the lecture world had begun to open up. *My Journey through Amazonia* was quite a good selling title in the mid-nineteen fifties, and a few Scottish societies invited me to appear on their syllabus. The colour slide of myself with Miss Universe caused local speculation, and one woman even asked Trudie whether or not she thought I 'might have kissed her' (Miss Universe).

A Scottish *Sunday Express* interview for the then Peter Dundas column had described me as using a 'long jade cigarette holder' (which was quite untrue); and, taking everything into consideration, it still astonishes me that the practice prospered or at least did not fall apart, especially when a glossy magazine said that I was 'another Scottish eccentric who is better known abroad than at home'. Indeed, very many patients told me how much easier it was to talk to a doctor with 'experience' (though whatever that exactly meant I never fully understood). To round things off, my lecture audiences said, or so chairmen quipped when introducing me, that I was better able than most to describe the human drama in distant countries because experience as a doctor had made me unusually observant and responsive to the importance of trends.

Meanwhile, and on a strictly professional level, both Alistair and I were faced with several other challenges.

National Health Service regulations allowed, and still allow a 'worker' to be off work for three days without a medical certificate and this, it seemed to us, was folly. The privilege was intended, we were told, to allow a person with a very minor difficulty to lie up for a couple of days without causing fuss. In practice, it really gave unlimited licence to dodge the column at regular intervals as I have said earlier in this book. We figure that the country was losing several millions of working hours *per annum* through this loop-hole and that too many people were shysters – yet it was impossible for us to do anything about

157

them. We had also discovered that if a man went sick on Monday he would probably be willing to return to our office on Friday or Saturday for a 'final' insurance certificate and go back to work on the following Monday. Given, of course, that his illness was trivial. But he might equally well have been fit to return, say on the Wednesday or Thursday. Yet he would never, just never, do so. The country was again losing countless hours through refusal of fit men to return to work before either the following Monday or 'the beginning of their next shift', and we calculated that in many cases an illness (*sic*) worth two or three days at home was often extended to ten or very much more.

Then came the rub! If we tried to force the person back by refusing to issue an 'intermediate certificate' he would either send in a penal night call, threaten to 'change his doctor' or threaten to report us to the Medical Practices Committee. In a few cases we were even menaced by a shop steward, who said that if we did not part with the required certificate not only would he and his family change to someone who would 'give lines without making bloody difficulties', or he would see to it that all members of his union who were on our list 'lifted their cards'.

This, of course, was blackmail. Yet it happened monthly, especially during our early days, and until we had weeded out a hard core of professional bullies or malingerers, industrial malcontents and new-style social parasites accustomed to the avuncular easy-ozy attitudes of 'old Doctor Anderson's' later years.

It was possible to refer malingerers to a medical referee, and there was provision on insurance certificates for a doctor to show that he wished this to be done. Unfortunately the referees were overworked and several weeks usually passed before a case could be dealt with through that channel. Since patients knew all about the delays, threat of being referred cut little ice. They usually wanted 'only' one or two or three weeks off work, and to go through the referee routine meant considerably longer unless a special request was phoned through as a matter of urgency. We were also irritated by the fact that men of this type would invariably 'win'. The welfare state was being abused on all counts and, as we saw it, the more our patients prospered the more they wanted.

Our slums were early removed, new housing was of good standard and multiple stores were supplying families with quality goods on the never-never. Wall-to-wall floor coverings began to replace carpet squares or rugs and more and more houses were equipped with modern kitchen equipment. Television was also becoming standard, more and more families were running a car, and even holiday traditions were changing by the early sixties as the Costa Brava or Majorca took over from Blackpool.

One patient, who lived *only* on social security, did an annual two-week cruise at the Tourist end of a P and O ship, and made a different circuit every year for upwards of eight years. Excuse was that no money was spent on other luxuries, bingo, tobacco or alcohol, which was true, but the house had quality wall-to-wall carpeting, above average price furniture paid for on the never-never, and no shortage of heating or food. I daily wondered what the Hunger Marchers of my childhood would have thought about the new Britain. It was becoming privileged beyond their wildest hopes. As an Osbert Lancaster cartoon said a few years later when two very old and thin men looked at a demonstration of prosperous looking strikers. 'Things have changed since our time.'

I had also become friendly with our local Member of Parliament, Malcolm MacPherson, who introduced me to Kenneth Robinson, then shadow Minister of Health. My theory was that if Kenneth Robinson could be sold at least some of our ideas as to what was wrong with the Health Service things might improve when Labour took office. He discussed the matter in depth and was sympathetic to arguments bearing upon reducing practice lists to a maximum of 2,500. He was also completely informed (or so he claimed) about abuses inherent in the three-days-off-with-full-wages and no-certificate-required setup. He was even more emphatic about abuses practised daily through routine certification of patients, many of whom did not require benefit, and I was encouraged to hope that when Labour did return to power with Mr Robinson as Minister of Health matters would be different. But it was not so. They changed in not one significant respect and abuses continued. If anything they became worse when appointments systems were eventually forced upon the profession: which, in effect, they were, by the middle to later sixties – though, to be fair, not by Kenneth Robinson.

My early Westminster visits with Malcolm MacPherson – a splendid man—did, however, enable me to over-hear two conversations which I have never forgotten. The first involved the late Aneurin Bevan, who was heard to claim, shortly before he took ill, that he was the only man alive who could control the trade unions. He said that when he became Prime Minister, as he expected to do one day, confrontation with the unions would become inevitable, and that he was the only man alive who had enough of their confidence to make them understand what was involved in running a country or was represented by the Labour movement as a whole. Years later I think of his words as other Labour and Tory leaders continue to show their own inability to cope.

The second conversation was more worrying. We were having lunch when a lady being taken round by her Member was introduced to people at my table and, when leaving, became unexpectedly eloquent. How comforting it was, she said, for a simple woman like herself to know that the country was in the hands of such wonderful gentlemen. My host and the Members around waited until she had gone and then laughed till the tears ran down their cheeks.

'Did the silly woman not realise,' said one, 'that we are all mediocrities? That if we had any real ability we would be pulling in big money from industry or somewhere?' A second voice went further. Didn't she realise that it was worse than that? 'We are in politics because we like publicity and pushing people around.' A third voice bellowed almost hysterically. 'Wasn't that funny? Did everyone realise that they were *all* publicity seeking mediocrities in politics for power?'

I found the scene blood-chilling, and left in thoughtful mood for the north, but again, when I think over the fifteen years or so which have passed since that particular luncheon I would not doubt anything said. For a breath of time these men knew a few seconds of near truth. I think that for one of them the shock provoked an attack of hysteria, and I shall not easily forget his crimson face running with tears as he laughed . . . and laughed . . . and laughed.

Even the trade unions, however, took second place in my

thoughts when something else broke during a Saturday afternoon. Grangemouth holds some important industrial complexes and a senior executive from one concern came to my house for help even although he was not a patient. He underlined that his problem was non-medical. It was, in fact, blackmail and industrial espionage. Various approaches, he said, had been made from time to time by people whom he believed to have extreme international left wing affiliations. He had lately been caught short in an affair with a girl and there were threats to expose him locally if he did not hand over certain information. For reasons which still baffle me, he felt that I was the only person around who might be competent to advise.

I disliked the story, distrusted the man and had a strong instinct to protect myself, so I suggested that he tell his family, notify his seniors in detail, contact his solicitor and advise British security, with whom contact could be made either through the police or his lawyer. He then broke down and wept. He actually gibbered with fear, and was one of the few people I have ever seen who turned grey-green with terror. His reactions convinced me that at least he was sincere, but even so I wanted no part of him. Extreme left wing (or extreme right wing) fanatics, with or without affiliations abroad, left me very cold. I would become involved only if the matter concerned myself, and concerned myself very deeply indeed. So, beyond dissertating at length about what I knew of methods used to winkle information out of people of importance and underlining the folly of being 'weak', I turned him away.

His fate remained an unsolved mystery until the early seventies when a Sunday newspaper gave fairly extensive cover to a man caught during a torrid sex orgy in a London house. The man was my executive of years earlier. Either he had not learned his lesson or else had been framed by his 'extreme left wing politicals' for slip-up or non-co-operation. It sounded sinister, especially since I had, by that time, learned a good deal more about another country and Moscow had become a special interest.

The story was written up in *Destination Moscow* and in *The Day Khruschev Panicked* after Trudie and I had gone to Russia in 1958 and a series of odd circumstances had led us to quite a number of top people within the Moscow scene. We also collected a world scoop through being allowed to photograph the interior of Moscow Kremlin when the whole complex of buildings was unexpectedly made available to us and we did our best with a camera which was scarcely adequate. Even so we collected several score important photographs and launched an international lecture tour using the title *Moscow and the Kremlin Palaces*. The lecture, oddly enough, led me to a meeting with an English lady who had met Rasputin and had a side-seat at his murder.

The travel book was factual. The lecture was also factual, though sensational at the time, and I remember halls in Holland where audiences were jam-packed right up to within two metres or so from the screen. *The Day Khruschev Panicked* was more tricky. It was a thriller *based upon fact*, but sensitive fact. Britain, however, chose to accept it as literally true and a Sunday paper crucified me across the centre pages, while an acid confrontation with the columnist arranged by Welsh television ended by my telling him that his piece had been 'a reflection not only upon his professional capacity, but upon the wisdom of the committee which had been so ill-advised as to appoint him'.

My area medical establishment was cross. I was, at that time, a member of the local B.M.A. committee and my old friend Ernest Morrison of Stirling took a dim view, though everything still hinged around the vexed question of name. Why didn't I do what Richard Gordon had done and use that pseudonym? I protected myself by double checking, through London, exactly to what licence I was entitled, and found that I could not, to date, be found guilty of 'advertising'. On the contrary, London agreed with me that it was the other way about, because what reasonable people would wish to join the list of a doctor who cavorted around the Kremlin or hobnobbed with old Bolsheviks and wild communists?

As a side-interest, the wife of the poet, Hugh MacDiarmid, during a P.E.N. evening promised me – perhaps in jest, or possibly to underline her disapproval – a public execution when the communists took over, which was an exciting prospect and fame indeed.

Bernard Newman, one of the world's foremost celebrity lecturers, then arranged for my name to go on the panel of Foyle's Lecture Agency in London, and it became a relief to have someone else plan bookings and negotiate fees on the lecture circuit.

Yet my patients remained loyal, and the practice continued, slowly, to expand. We countered this by taking on a third partner so that our individual list still averaged out at around fifteen hundred patients each. Andrew Taylor became our number three and it would, I suppose, have been hard to find more dissimilar individuals. Andrew was around the same age as my brother, but introverted, quiet, slow moving, pale faced, over-conscientious and very thoughtful. So far as I know he had no especial feelings about patients or medicine, one way or the other, and he accepted practice problems as they arose. He was a good doctor, and respected. It was tragic when he was forced to retire and then die with a coronary only a dozen years later and when still in his middle forties.

Alistair was also a good doctor, and not only respected but beloved. Probably none of his patients even guessed how much he hated doing medicine, or how much he detested life in Grangemouth, or how particularly he felt at odds with local sensibilities and totems. In short, he loathed the place and burned himself up with indignation at everything around: the ruthlessness of unions, the bad workmanship of some tradesmen who, as patients, screwed the last ounce of service from their doctors, the hypocrisy of a smug mid-middle class, the continual agitation for more, and more, of everything, the way in which money ran out after one week of any strike, and our own need to try and persuade certain stores not to take back articles sold on the never-never from patients because of non-payment. He particularly disapproved the wishy-washy approach of churchmen to social problems. In fact he had underlined this by having his own children christened and baptised within the Episcopal church, than which few insults could be greater from a member of the Church of Scotland. Yet he wore a mask from morning till night, seldom aggressed and had the patience of Job.

I, by contrast, lived in a state of perpetual minor aggression against shysters and all who were abusing the State on virtually

163

every count. I took satisfaction only from knowing that at least my patients realised where they stood with me, that there was no mask, and that if they did not like me they could lump me. I was too busy to worry over-much about whether they liked me or not. Life was full, and I had got temporarily quit of bloody dreams and threatening scalpels, but I was still forced to accept that even family doctoring was possible only because of other activities which provided release from tension. I too disliked my work but for that very reason I was compelled by conscience (as Alistair was) to give nothing but my ultimate best. I also lived in fear that I might become careless simply because I detested the job, which was probably all rather silly.

I particularly disliked many people who wished to be treated as private patients. When asked why they felt that this might be a better arrangement their response was almost always the same. They appeared to believe that I would give better treatment because I was paid a better fee. Nor did they seem to realise what a monstrous insult it was to suggest that any *conscientious* doctor would grade, as it were, the quality of his services according to fiscal return (though many of the less conscientious did, and do!). When they had explained that they wanted 'better treatment' I always outlined how I had a contract with the state, that my state patients came first, that I would accept the person as 'private' only if he appreciated that even if it came to an emergency involving, for the sake of argument, a state patient and himself, that the state person would be handled first. I also made the point that I saw private patients only after completing all work bearing upon my state flock and that this would normally mean consultation in the very late evening, probably around nine or ten o'clock.

None ever appreciated this argument and normally they went elsewhere.

If, however, the new-arrival said that he wished 'to go private' because he preferred not to sit in the waiting-room, or because he was elderly or shy, or with an embarrassing health problem, then I did accept him; but I finished, in the end, with only one private family, a couple of real quality whom I much respected.

It was also interesting to discover how reluctant most private patients were to pay bills. One man, in fact, and a person of some local importance, was so enraged when given our account for one hundred guineas after weekly attention for a year, that he visited my office and was restrained from breaking up the furnishings only with difficulty. He was eventually accepted by another doctor who later told me, in effect, that since the man's condition was largely due to drinking a bottle of whisky every night it seemed reasonable to charge him realistically, but that we had made the mistake of tendering a bill before he died and that men of his type expected the doctor's account to be paid only when winding up their estate and not before. Service in life to be paid for only after death appeared to be the slogan. It was a novel way of dealing with accounts which failed to appeal, and we wrote the thing off to experience.

This man is also burned in memory for one other reason. A Saturday afternoon 'urgent' call brought me to his house, where I found him wearing only a pyjama top and smoking cap. He was squatting half way upstairs and had defaecated generously upon the carpet. He registered resentment by throwing a hefty turd which missed my head but struck the door, bespattering shoulder and right cheek with offence. He had ammunition enough for two more shots, and it was no consolation to remember that he was an elderly alcoholic, a life-long tyrant towards most who surrounded him and a creature with neither grace nor distinction.

One other private patient experience during our cabbage days still makes us smile. The couple concerned had insisted on private facilities, and used them freely. When our account was sent in after the first six months they explained that it had all been a terrible mistake, that they had, all the time, been state patients, and that neither could understand how the confusion could have come about. So they, too, dodged the column, and we had not the heart to remind them of how they had invariably rubbed in their private status when seeking advice. So sad really ... yet so funny too!

One thing seems certain, however. There is still a vast difference between Scots and English in their approach to doctors. My work on the lecture circuit has brought me into repeated contact with many practitioners all over England and gossipy exchanges have made me very certain that this is so. Professional experience with 'English' patients living in the North has also confirmed these tentative conclusions made at second hand.

Too many Scots tend to be demanding, ruthless, inconsiderate, and frequently either unappreciative or unwilling to show appreciation. The English are much less demanding, more intelligent in their approach to illness, worry less and co-operate better. They are also more civilised in their general attitudes and show more appreciation.

Scots revel in the myth that they are 'blunt', 'no-nonsense types', 'no-time-for-sentiment men', 'know-where-you-stand-with-us-sort-of-people', or 'take-us-as-you-bloody-find-us families', and affect to despise a non-regional accent, ordinary formal civilities and much which is gracious in routine living, while the English appear, without even trying, to be more cultivated.

The Irish are worse than Scots on every count, but one must add the bland persuasiveness, suave conceit, apparently plausible prejudices and general blarney which makes confrontation tiresome or routine professional contact slightly wearing.

As for the Welsh! Sing-song accents and vaguely fussy attitudes, bland faces and expectant eyes, plaintive excuses and longing to do-the-right-thing remind me of children, but like so many other lovable children they, too, can pack a punch, as I learned from bitter experience throughout the years. My choices were English, Welsh, Scots and Irish in that order, and I often envied English colleagues who seemed to live in dreamland.

As time went on, however, I began to detect a new phenomenon. Unions were developing the blackmail technique against society to boost wages, and many men, especially dockers and members of the Transport and General Workers Union, made no secret of the fact that they knew what was happening and figured that blackmail with violence would pay bigger dividends than reasonable negotiation, yet did not realise how, by admitting this across my desk they were also tending to prove that they knew what they were doing when handling their doctors along the same lines.

Heedless, staring, lustful eyes
look out from heads bereft of thought,
While grasping hands, all grace forgot
and voices shrill with rage
demand their rights.

'Workers demand the right to work!'
A slogan based on a cunning lie!
Money they want! A mob, work-shy,
Gadarene-like stream
Downhill to endless fights.

Greed their curse, their spirits dead
to every thought but money gain!
Hate-men the In-men!
Violent vicious venom
corrupts their souls, and gainful
days turn now to soulless nights.

Such people admitted freely to myself that they used overtime
to complete what they could easily have done within normal
hours and many seemed to suspect that doctors too gave less
than their best. Many found it difficult to understand that
nothing extra could be winkled out of a decent doctor through
threats or cunning. Many seemed convinced that if they blustered
enough they would get, for example, extra tablets on a prescription; or that if the doctor promised a repeat visit on Friday he
could be browbeaten into making one on Wednesday or Thursday as well; or that if two hours elapsed between putting in
a standard-type call and the doctor arriving it might be cut
to one hour next time if the wretched practitioner was bullied
enough into feeling that he must not again keep that family
waiting for two hours. It was all a progressively increasing
trend, and demand for treatment was being made where none
would actually have been considered even a few years earlier.
A mild corn might be good for some days off work. A standard
summer cold could win a week. A slight flare up of dyspepsia
on Sunday morning could justify an emergency Sunday call.
A child with a slight temperature on Saturday night would
ustify a late night call yet, and this staggered me, find the

parents who had requested it *refuse* to seek out a chemist to make up the script and wait until Sunday. Nor were such people particularly exceptional, though they were most common in the late twenty to forty-five age group, and they were usually earning biggish money.

Teenagerers and young adults were my easiest and most co-operative patients, and the age-gap became unimportant once they accepted that I was sincere, possibly biased towards new generations' ways of thinking, and prepared to listen to everything or anything they cared to tell me. Their biggest tragedy, it seemed to me, was that most of them desperately wanted to be approved by their parents, yet could seldom find any common ground for conversation in depth. The gulf was just as deep as it had been when I was the same age. It began to disappear only among those younger parents, whom I began to see rearing their own families over the last few years before I finally withdrew – which is why I feel that the final death-knell of 19th century brand of family stresses rang out only during a late-mid 20th century when an enraged middle-aged tribe began to scream 'permissive society' at boys and girls who wished only to avoid repeating or continuing the mistakes of their elders. As I judged them, they were sufficiently courageous to demand that these elders justify attitudes which seemed either foolish or illogical, and I admired their technique when faced with the real possibility of global destruction because of these very elders or others like them in several countries. They did the only thing possible when they stated a simple total solution: 'make love, not war'.

Social historians have yet to record how a generation reacted to the knowledge that it might not live to become grandparents, and when it was confronted by daily risk of destruction because of an ultimate weapon devised by men and women who had never been able to devise means to live at peace. Their simple solution, to make love and not war, seems a logical and complete answer. If all the world responded the ultimate weapon would cease to matter. Perhaps their solution was too simple!

I also felt increasingly frustrated on all sides by the enormous blanket of problems which seemed to smother so much that was capable of being good, but I had acquired an especial contempt for people who used political threats to make me toe their own particular line.

My first crisis of this sort broke when the son of a prominent local political figure, a man of neither ability, character nor capacity, but still a power in the town because of his 'union' involvements, got entangled with a girl. She threatened to charge him with assault and the matter dropped into my hands during an evening clinic. I decided that the patient was 'dangerous' and wished to refer him to a local psychiatric clinic. His reaction to this advice was so pathological that I decided, instead, to have him 'certified', but to do so required signature from a second doctor not connected with our practice and I was astounded that no local practitioner approached would touch the matter when they heard who was involved. I then called in a member of the public health staff, but he, too, refused to co-operate. The patient's father, I was told, could ruin him.

Meanwhile the patient's father had spent some time making that very point clear to myself. If I 'certified' his son he would take every trade union member away from our firm's list, or so he blustered. I then gave the father a choice. Either he persuaded his son to enter hospital as a voluntary patient or I would call in the police and allow the girl to press charges. She had co-operated with me to date, and I knew that she would continue to do so. Meanwhile I had to protect the public, and since the son was a menace he either went behind bars or into hospital. Father could make a choice. The end point was that the old man knuckled down, and next morning a taxi removed the son to much needed treatment, but the incident proved that there were no limits to which a little man might go when thwarted, nor had I any illusions about his union threat. His influence was such that at least a proportion of the men would string along with him.

When discussing this type of situation with other family doctors I began to appreciate the mistakes I was making. None with whom I discussed our tactics would have allowed such a situation to develop. They came to terms with events and avoided confrontations, and they disagreed with my policies saying that I did not like the colour grey. Doctors had not been responsible for making crazy regulations which enabled patients to con the

State. Nor were they responsible for delays in referring shysters to the Medical Referee. Life was life, was life, was life! Take things as they come, they advised me. You can't keep back the tides, and there was nothing any of us could do to improve laws which made it possible, not only to be protected from cradle to the grave, but to draw social security for a concubine or use social security to finance a P and O cruise, a motor car or weekly sessions at bingo. So why bother? Live and let live. There were enough coronaries around without my adding to them. After all, I made a living, didn't I? And the question was a bad joke!

But the doctors were not victims of state parsimony only during early days; they have been victims of state folly on several counts right through from the beginning, and their status has annually been lowered until many patients felt that they could manipulate them at will to win that slip of paper which is really a cheque for hard cash.

My own 'white-papers' for the cure of many ills found no response on either medical or political fronts.

I believed, and still believe, that every new patient arriving in any area should be given one full year from first becoming a householder or paying rent, during which he would be entitled to 'use' any doctor he chose and contact one or all as he wished. If he had no occasion to ask for medical help he would still be able to assess at least what the public thought about individual doctors, but after one year he would be obliged to join the list of any particular firm of his own choice. Having done so, he would *not* thereafter be granted permission to transfer until he had justified his case in writing to members of a tribunal to be appointed in every medical zone. His doctor, of course, would be able to state the argument from another angle and be able, for the first time, to issue certificates (which are really cheques for cash) thinking *solely* in terms of medical requirements. Nor would this remove a patient's right to choose his own doctor. He would have a whole year in which to finalise choice; and he would still be able to transfer if his complaint was valid, but he would *not* be able to switch simply because of a feud about 'certificates' which were not justified by a health problem. 'Blackmail techniques' would be eliminated.

During the year when the patient might receive service from

any local doctor the practitioner would be paid on a system similar to that controlling treatment of 'temporary residents', and there would be no administrative problem. My approach also suggested removal of any discrimination between family and hospital doctors, would put them on the same salary scale and have a proportion of family doctors given full consultant status along lines similar to those followed in the hospital service.

This approach to the future would also insist upon equality in division of 'merit awards' between peripheral hospitals, teaching centres and family doctors, but special fiscal 'prizes' having no bearing upon superannuation, would be given to those very few men of immense capacity and distinction who do valid pioneer work and important research. For example, Andrew Logan's achievement in transplanting lungs and heart would qualify when taken into consideration with all his other achievements in establishing a world famous thoracic unit, as would any consultant in any branch of the profession who was clearly responsible for a major advance in his own subject. The prize would be something realistic, like twenty or twenty-five thousand pounds, be tax free, and given as a once-and-for-all, *only* to men who satisfied exacting criteria. It would *not* be enough simply to hold down a chair or run any standard unit. 'Contribution to human progress' would be the overriding essential, and this would, in practice, involve only people with international reputations whose work had been generally accepted. Until the present merit award system has been removed there can only be tensions between various interests within the profession.

As for salary, there is now so much rule-of-thumb about medical humdrumery that skills which used to be rated essential have become less necessary. A really expert clinical diagnostician is now a rare treasure. The normal approach is to lay the suspect patient on to a conveyor belt which will take him through a series of tests and end by establishing a diagnosis (the machine medicine of Sir Robert Muir).

Professor Harrington's teachings still hold good in spite of modern techniques, and many patients still die because of a 'negative' stomach X-ray. Not all such X-rays reveal all malignancies, and how many minor or early coronaries are still missed by family doctors or physicians who do use an electrocardiograph?

On the surgical side much less skill is required today than in the pre-antibiotic, pre-transfusion, pre-all-sorts era; and post-operative wound sepsis is too common *in spite of* antibiotics. I cannot see that such men as these merit increase in salary.

Family doctors are now far from the bread-line but it is still unfair that men prepared to keep their lists at a realistic figure of 2,000 patients or less earned, even after 1972, proportionately too little by comparison with others. During earlier days the differential was enormous, and in 1955 my own nett income from an apparently prosperous medical practice was only £1,432 – which was monumentally unrealistic when matched against services given. During 1957 my own nett practice income was £1,393, *a reduction* in personal earnings because we were employing and paying for our own ancillary staff in order to raise standards.

Given that we increased our list in order to boost income, standards were certain to fall, as they have now fallen for most family doctors who operate the appointments system even in relation to a list of around 2,800 to 3,000. Time per patient has been sliced to four or five minutes by this imposition, and many doctors cope only by reducing time passed in examinations, keeping case records or discussing problems and by off loading as much as possible to hospital out-patient clinics. Others refer every problem which does not respond rapidly to blitz therapy with a 'wonder-drug' to the hospital conveyor belt. Antibiotics and emotion-adjusting drugs take care of another proportion, and, if tension still continues, a 'functional diagnosis' tab can be tagged on as a preliminary to handling victims along traditional lines, since there is said to be no time to pursue conversations in depth until the cause of stress has been exposed.

Sensitive practitioners now live in conflict, and more develop tension diseases annually, while thick-skinned types who can rationalise their situation through elastic consciences buy larger cars, keep more and more to office hours, off-load night work on to juniors and compromise on everything. Yet patients usually recover, thanks to 'wonder drugs' which have worked more wonders than most patients dream of and which have enabled very small men to walk tall in public.

I was not surprised when my brother began to show signs of wishing to quit the whole complicated business and earn his living as a full-time author. He had more or less continual broncho-spasm which required daily therapy. Most of his patients were more fit than their doctor, but he still continued to wear his mask and struggled on for a little while longer. He lost *not one* working day in ten years when many hundreds of our patients suffering from the same disabilities had lost a total of many months. It was, of course, purely a question of character!

My own problems, however, were not simple either. Income was impossibly low, but boosted through lecturing, writing, and a little medical journalism. It would have been comparatively simple to allow our medical list to increase, but we all accepted that to do so meant reduction in efficiency. Consultations lasting twenty minutes or more would become a thing of the past and our relationship with patients would be debased. There would also be a clash of conscience and need to accept a burden of guilt which none of us were prepared to carry. So we struggled on, handicapped by alarming overdrafts and secret sorrows that we could not give as much as we wished to wives or families.

My journeys to fulfil talking engagements became downright stupid and I would sometimes leave home in the late evening after a long day's work and evening clinic to motor as far as, for example, Huddersfield or Leeds, Blackpool or Lincoln in order to fulfil a luncheon date next day. If I was fortunate there would be a second lecture commitment in the evening and I would return home at dawn having again motored through the night. Nor were roads fast, since the motorway system was only a twinkle in the planners' eyes. It was all rather foolish and I dare say I must have been tough to have done it.

Yet this release from medicine made professional life tolerable. That, and the travel background to my talks which led to us programming at least one long and exciting trip every year. We had also invested savings in a second house in Perthshire and escaped there on any weekend when I could be off-duty. Our second home was magnificently located within a large estate to which we had full access, and long hill walks may also have helped to undo damage to health of which I was increasingly conscious. Occasional dreams still oppressed me. I was even afraid that I would aggress against some particularly unreasonable patient. I reacted badly to night work and had become an early insomniac. My weight was a stone below normal and I could become irritable even with Trudie who, more than ever, was my right hand and most precious treasure.

I had enough sense to know that when a man began to abuse his own cherished treasure something was very far wrong. Yet I had a curious instinct that Destiny was still presenting me with a series of challenges and that it was important for me to accept them until something, obviously 'intended', signposted my path to another destination. Signs of stress, however, were beginning to engrave upon my face and Trudie sensed that I was becoming self-conscious. With her usual incredible 'awareness' of my phobias and vanities she wrote a few lines and left them by my plate at breakfast time on Christmas morning.

Lines

Lines of goodness – lines of kindness –
Lines of knowledge – lines of care –
Lines of character and laughter!
These are lines be proud to wear.

Were there none I sure would wonder –
'has this man no signs to show
What his Maker had intended
Me and all the world to know?'

As you are I'll always love you.
No amount of lines will bring
Less affection, love or pleasure.
Let happiness be reigning King.
                                        Trudie Mair

Her reassurance did much to bring my attitudes and standards of value into focus. Practice problems became less important. Trudie and the boys were my top priority. They and my flirtation with Destiny were my sheet anchors while Trudie, in her own right, gave, as she had always given, so much pleasure that it almost frightened me. Where, I sometimes began to ask myself, would I be without her?

Health apart we were battling against yet one other odd problem within the practice, and the question of prescription costs was seldom far from mind, a situation so absurd that we began to understand why *Alice in Wonderland* is a favourite British classic.

14 HOW NOT TO HANDLE DRUGS

An interesting black market occasionally operated locally but I discovered it only by chance when a cantankerous docker complained bitterly that his rheumatism was not improving even after prolonged treatment with cortisone and other appropriate drugs. He was then in bed with influenza but had been receiving maintenance doses of tablets monthly for several years. I guessed that he was campaigning for adjustment in treatment and decided to check up on how much cortisone was left from previous prescriptions.

He said that they were finished but became aggressive when I asked to see the bottle. It became obvious that something off-beat was going on and I went over the house with a fine tooth-comb until I located it behind a massive clock in the living-room. One bottle held over 500 cortisone tablets while beside it there was a container with 24 penicillin V capsules issued weeks earlier to someone else in the family. There were also 1,000 codeine tablets or more, also collected over the previous six months, two issues of a birth control script normally given to his daughter, and sixty sleeping and pain relieving tablets called sonalgin.

He eventually admitted that he was about to clinch a dock-side deal with a high feed-back price for everything including the codeines, which, he thought, were sold in Karachi as fertility remedies for men. This man earned big money, and he did have some rheumatism, yet he had used little or no treatment prescribed by hospital, had dosed himself with aspirin and Sloan's liniment and sold his drugs through his own black market. He dealt with one vessel only, where a Pakistani contact was said to be reliable, and he claimed that he had the right to do what he wanted with anything he 'bought' – meaning the cover-charge per prescription.

As a result of this and other similar situations, I tried, but again with no success, to persuade the Organisation into giving every patient a receipt showing the actual cost to the tax-payer for every script made up by a chemist. This seems a simple enough thing to arrange and a worth-while step in educating people towards appreciating the cost of drugs, but it took a few more years of experience to show why the Organisation refused to wear it.

A doctor known to prescribe consistently pricey medicines might become known to patients, who would almost certainly compare costs of their various treatments, and doctors might decide that it paid off in expanding their lists to use expensive drugs. While, in real fact, government put out a lot of time and money into reducing prescribing costs, and the government's campaign opened with a report from a group called the Douglas Committee which began by saying:

'The Douglas Committee has seen how some doctors with persistently high costs . . . whose actions must have a serious inflationary effect upon the costs of doctors *anxious to retain their patients*, go for years without any serious attempt made to investigate their costs.'

In effect, government was afraid that practitioners who prescribed top quality medicine might influence patients away from those who used something less and so took steps to protect inferior persons – which seemed, from any point of view, re-markable, especially since costly treatment frequently reduced time off work (given that patients co-operated properly) and thereby actually *reduced* costs within other branches of the N.H.S.

Methods adopted to investigate prescribing costs were *apparently* reasonable, but, in fact, they simply would not have stood up to any dispassionate study.

A flimsy reached us all at regular intervals and listed certain figures: they bore upon drugs prescribed around a year earlier but included *average* cost of each script issued by the doctor named, average cost for the *area* in which he practised and the *national* average. If an individual's average was found to be significantly more than the area average the doctor was liable to be summoned before a committee and required to explain why.

Under certain circumstances officials could, and did, *deduct* the excess from his next salary cheque.

It follows that many doctors studied their drug costs most carefully, and that *there followed a general tendency to use the cheaper medicines*. An 'area' holding even a few men still using a 'coloured water routine' clearly had a low average figure, by comparison with which a conscientious practitioner giving quality drugs would personally contrast unfavourably.

Bearing in mind the average practitioner's tendency to avoid confrontations with authority, his reluctance to have his salary trimmed, and the fact that cases of practitioners who had been 'fined' were given at least medical publicity, most doctors toed a governmental line which aimed at keeping costs down irrespective of total over-all efficiency, and there was little or nothing they could do about it. My own firm was summoned to appear before the local committee on one occasion only. The meeting was acid and I like to think that I covered my own feelings on the matter with sufficient clarity that no one was left in doubt as to how we would react if we were bothered again. But it was a nuisance-experience and made me more anti-Organisation than ever, even if we were not fined, but let off, so to speak, with a caution.

We altered our habits in no respect, however, but continued to give our people the best drugs available, and I decided, with my brother, to resign at once if we were again criticised on this count. We felt that we were answerable only to our consciences. We were confident that our families would not starve even if we did quit medicine, and we refused to have our professional decisions as to what was correct treatment discussed at a distance either by lay-men, or by colleagues, some of whom were themselves indifferent physicians. The very fact that they sat on this committee also suggested that they were 'establishment men', and thus likely to be prejudiced.

But we were far from being off the hook, patients too, were difficult about scripts, and complained bitterly when required to pay a few pence according to the ups and downs of varying state regulations, though our problems arose especially with people who simply would not follow advice. A truly incredible number of patients stopped taking antibiotic courses whenever their health began to improve, and it was both time-consuming and monotonous having to explain to each and every one the importance of completing the course. Few seemed (or seem today), to understand that no doctor worth his salt issued more of anything through any script than was required, and that they had a total obligation to complete treatment unless modified after discussion with the doctor. Indeed there must be hundreds of thousands of pounds worth of drugs always lying around Britain which *should* have been used but have been 'stopped' because people *felt* that they were no longer necessary. The loss is a steady drain on the tax-payer.

One result has also been to increase enormously the total number of resistant bacteria in the world, and to make treatment, even with wonder-drugs, increasingly unpredictable. Yet there is no way of disciplining persons who abuse the service in this way and *no attempt has been made to educate them*. Although a proportion might behave differently if they knew the actual costs involved, no steps have been taken to make even this possible, while attack on reducing doctors' costs has been uninspired, if not foolish and very biased.

Government, in fact, by its heavy-handed approach has even encouraged many doctors to give only the barest minimal number of antibiotics on any script, especially if cost is on the high side, and only too often the course given is actually *less* than what is considered essential. Humanity has really only been able to keep a step or two ahead of disaster because research chemists have, so far, been able to produce new antibiotics every few months. When ingenuity and possibilities have finally been exhausted the world may yet see a return to 'the old days', and I do not imagine that broad spectrum therapy can continue to be developed indefinitely.

As for drugs! Imagination boggles.

The world may not realise how many people are now kept going because of 'maintenance therapy'. Our brush with the Organisation concerning prescribing costs triggered us into investigating, over a thirteen week period, exactly how many, and what type of scripts were issued. The results (*British Medical Journal*, Nov. 12, 1960, 1442) are interesting, bearing in mind that Grangemouth was still Scotland's boom-town, that there was minimal poverty, good housing, almost full employment and, in theory at least, every opportunity for people to be relaxed.

Yet out of 4,701 patients seen within our offices during the 13 week period, 2,091 or 44·4% required maintenance treatment of one sort or another, while 749, or 37·06% of 2,021 cases visited at their own home also required maintenance therapy. We took these figures even further and proved that 19·83% of our entire practice was on maintenance treatment of one sort or another, and of that 20% (19·83%), 51·87% were suffering from stress diseases. Which works out at approximately 10% of our list. This is, in fact, a low estimate, because it does not include a large number of suspect people suffering from conditions *believed*, but not proven, also to be due to tension. It is even more interesting that although 40·78% of people seen during that 13 week period were on maintenance therapy they used 52% of all prescriptions issued, while the 10% of stressed people used 28·5% of all scripts issued. In other words, *almost one third of prescriptions issued were angled to cope with the results of tension*. So much, we felt, for life in the boom-town. The emotions, too were booming, boom-aboom-boomzimbo! In conflict? Why?

Within twenty years of the N.H.S. being launched, Britain had, like most other advanced countries, been converted into a nation of drug dependents. Long-term treatment using barbiturates or other emotion-manipulating chemicals became standard. Call it 'addiction' or call it 'psychological dependence' and it is the same thing in the end. Millions of sedatives, tranquillisers, stimulants, or anti-depressants were swallowed annually and the whole situation was seemingly socially and morally acceptable.

Little wonder that society pounced on a miniscule minority of inadequate people who became involved in the so-called drug scene of the later 60s. Society loves a whipping-boy as much as it loves a scapegoat and society found satisfaction in ventilating its (then) own guilt sense against a very tiny number who really harmed few but themselves.

The permissive society never did equate with a 'drug society', but the welfare state did, very swiftly, equate with a drug situation which mattered. Tax-payers supplied the money. Patients supplied the pressure and demands. Doctors supplied the scripts.

Research chemists provided new methods of juggling with emotions, and popular articles in press or other news media justified everything. Any old-hat ideas of 'finding the root-cause of an emotional problem' became unpopular, especially with doctors, since it was much more simple to prescribe wonder drugs for mood-swings than to sit through repeated sessions and try to treat basic causes of need.

Addiction is also a curious thing. One bachelor patient was totally dependent every night upon eating one quarter pound of chocolate peppermint creams before being able to sleep. On several occasions he forgot to buy his wretched sweets and sent in a night-call at around one in the morning, when I would find him with typical drug-withdrawal signs which responded immediately to a couple of peppermint creams. I learned to keep a box or two at home to meet the emergency, but ended by removing him from our list when the man became a total nuisance. But so much for addiction or dependence. These problems can develop in regard to almost anything.

Abuse of drugs could also be used to end a patient's life, and more than one apparently respectable woman kept life-saving drugs *away* from husband or elderly patient when they had reached the end of their patience.

I accepted that I seemed to be incident-prone, and did not too much like it. Being accident-prone is bad enough, but to be incident-prone is worse, though one patient from whom I had few secrets suggested a possible reason for my incident-packed life.

I was now accepted by many as a professional traveller, and had become involved with lesser-known Turkey. My book *Doctor in Turkey* had raised some local interest, and people had begun to ask more seriously how my wife and I could possibly identify or be happy with people of such different tradition and background.

Some also knew that I had, after quite a short time, quit being a member of the local Marriage Guidance Council, and a few even knew why, since it was very understandable. The council, so far as I could understand policy, saw unhappy people only by appointment – which was absurd, as I discovered after listening to the well-intentioned group pontificating about a patient

181

whose problem was familiar to myself. Her husband, however, belonged to another practice and had refused to see me. It was he who had gone to the marriage guidance experts (*sic*) for advice, and as I listened I felt that this was the end of the road. They refused to visit the house, but set up appointments for a later date. None could understand that trouble existed only because the girl was tall, her kitchen sink at too low a level, and that she had a continually painful back from washing-up. Her husband refused to replace the sink unit and the housing authorities to rehouse her, so relationships had perished on that cluster of rocks and I was certain that all would be well given that the family was either rehoused or the husband persuaded to replace the kitchen unit. This practical solution cut no ice, and we were thigh deep in theory about all manner of irrelevant emotional side-issues when I went home to type a letter of resignation. The Marriage Guidance Council, from my limited experience, could fail because it refused to visit the battlefields during battles and was coy about discussing sex in depth. From my point of view it was waste of time. I achieved more as a 'loner' because it seemed that a solid number of people were willing to open up their hearts to myself in private simply because I did have a varied experience of odd places and off-beat people which might make my opinion marginally more significant than anything open from other sources.

But there were exceptions, and I discovered exactly how significant the press could be when I began to contribute a regular medical column in a Scottish newspaper. The column was, of course, anonymous, but it became invaluable. I might find a really tiresome patient who would believe nothing and quibble either about treatment or advice given. If, however, I brought him back two weeks later after having written up a piece to fit my own requirements I was home and dry. 'Extraordinary' I would say, 'Saw a piece in so-and-so the other day about what we were discussing last visit. Have a look.'

That column could erase almost any difficulty since, for most of my doubting Thomases, the written word was final. Armed with a column I realised that a man could make some people believe almost anything, though curiously enough I never related this to how people might react towards my own books. I did not know that my Khruschev thriller had caused various people to identify me with certain episodes or to say: 'It's just like what he would have said to yon man.'

I did not even anticipate public reaction when I launched my first orthodox spy thriller in 1963. Ian Fleming had died and a question had arisen: who would be the new Bond? This was finally decided by marching feet striding towards the libraries to borrow Len Deighton's anti-heroes, but there was an evening when the matter was thrashed out on television with Cliff Michelmore. Len Deighton with myself (the short leet, so to speak) read parts of our works, and *Death's Foot Forward* launched my man, David Grant, into a lesser orbit. A pen and ink drawing of Grant even appeared in a Sunday newspaper and serial rights were bought for four figures. An American and other editions followed, but I never realised that I would, by various people, be identified with my own hero. How dumb can one be? I had made the man a doctor, he had opted out of medicine, he was from the Edinburgh area, he had become a cosmopolitan, and, to round matters off, his colouring was too much like my own for general comfort. Talk about the subconscious interfering when writing a book! It is surprising that only a very few left the practice because, as I was given to understand, David Grant's love life was so colourful that they could not tolerate further association with myself. Curiously enough, one family also left because of a 'Doctor Alistair's' book. This time because religious sensibilities had been ruffled by my brother's pen.

Of course, I was again asked by one particular senior to stop using my own name and I myself added the chorus this time: 'Why don't you do as Richard Gordon did? He used a pseudonymn.' But I was adamant. It was high time, I felt, that the British Medical Association got itself more accurately into focus with the times. Anyhow, sundry top names had done very nicely, thank you, in the way of generating personal publicity of a different order, and using it to attract patients, while anything I did was more likely to operate in the reverse direction.

Meanwhile established trends continued, and I remained knee-deep or waist-high in other people's problems.

A recurring mystery had centred around many strange

decisions by housing factors and local authorities until I was eventually able to predict with 99% accuracy which teenager, when married, would return from the honeymoon to a new house, and I could equally predict which individualists would not quickly be rehoused. It would be extremely improper were I to suggest that there was graft, corruption, improper allocation or the faintest impropriety. I only know that it would have taken a deal of eloquence and presentation of facts to convince me that there was not.

Most of the council were no better than the local people deserved, since only a minority turned out to vote at municipal elections, and I was weekly reminded, for some reason or other, of my father's oft repeated statement that he had never yet met either an intelligent or educated councillor. Grangemouth was Scotland's boom-town chiefly because of oil, but I did not forget an oil magnate who told me in Greece: 'We don't discuss things with local authorities, and we seldom discuss them even with government, except to go through the motions at top level. Look boy. We are oil and *we tell them.*' When he knew my address he grinned. 'Canute couldn't stop the tides. When the first refinery was opened in Grangemouth nothing anyone could do could ever have stopped, modified, or altered a thing. People like *us* made Grangemouth. Not your council.'

This may or may not have been so, but where it was possible for a small man to pitch his weight about at low level local councillors pitched it good, and allocation of houses seemed to make chaos out of confusion. Some of my people suffered badly. Not once, from beginning to end of my time in the area, was I able to organise rehousing for deserving patients except in the one dramatic case of the haunted council house, which I did handle with kid gloves, and with such discretion that I won through. The same technique could never have been used twice.

1963 became an important year. My second spy thriller, *Miss Turquoise*, was accepted by my publishers; Trudie and I escorted a party from the Royal Scottish Geographical Society round various archaeological sites in Anatolia; we rented a chalet for a month near Goldiwil, our favourite Swiss village; we gave our first lectures on board one of P and O's luxury summer cruises and covered the port situations in Barcelona, Crete and Athens;

occasional television spots continued: the lecture circuit became more commanding; and, to round matters off, Alistair had retired a year earlier. It was our first year without a quality partner. The challenges of practice work had gone sour when matched against the absurdities which governed Britain's National Health Service, but in particular Alistair had found it disagreeable to continue in a situation where he was, *ex officio*, virtually compelled to condone the actions of many who were really swindling the state. Welfare had run riot, and with it greed had become a vampire which was beginning to drain not only the life blood, but the very character of the country. Standing on one's own two feet was no longer fashionable. It was not even necessary.

My brother figured that life in Appin, close to his favourite islands, might do something to heal many scars.

He was much beloved, or so we understood, by several thousand patients who signified their appreciation by giving donations sufficient to enable Jenny Hutchison, our valued receptionist, to buy a low-cost tape recorder and hand over a cheque for twenty-odd pounds. Most of the money came from less than 2% of our list and we found the situation amusing. I was very certain that when my own time came I would exit at speed, and that there would be no time for either ceremony or discussion.

Only two things prevented me from following his example there and then. It would have been a shoddy trick to have left Andrew Taylor in the lurch and faced with need to collect two new partners. It would have been equally shoddy to have confronted my parents with a double disappointment. They were able to accept that Alistair had left medicine because of persistent bronchospasm (asthma) since childhood, and that it was sensible to live in the pure, clean air of Argyll; but the fact remained that it was a bitter pill to swallow, and I knew that I must wait awhile before distressing them any more.

They were fit as fleas, alert, mobile, cavorting all over the countryside in a biggish car, and seemingly set for the century. I even began to think that they might 'see me out first'. Nor had I been completely forgiven for quitting surgery. I had become *only* a G.P.

The fact that I was happily married to a wonderful wife and mother seemed unimportant. The fact that we seemed to be building a good relationship with our children was never mentioned. My parents perhaps never even noticed that my wife was happy, that we had a valued circle of friends and that we had all been blessed, for years, with good health and a sense of humour. We had to accept that our values were no longer their values and that their gods no longer could find places among our gods. They took comfort only in trying to persuade themselves that at least it was not every G.P. who was also a lecturer and author, but for the most part I was not forgiven. I was still, basically, *only* a family doctor.

Standards are interesting things!

15 ESCAPE

Alistair returned as required to let me continue on the lecture circuit or to cover my expanding travel interests, especially with P and O lines. P and O-ing was a tremendous experience, and during our busiest period Trudie and I did seven lecture cruises in two seasons, but we also met patients in unexpected places, some of whom were noted for putting on the poor mouth back home: which was all very thought-provoking, especially since their skill as slick operators in the social security fields was familiar to myself. All, in fact, except one woman and one family were 1970s-style parasites able to manipulate the State because of idealistically conceived laws which took no count of human frailty. The lives of my patients had changed dramatically in less than fifteen years!

Death had become especially unpopular, though Catholics still died more or less graciously, and atheists, like agnostics, did not usually seem to have strong emotions, but Presbyterians fussed and took it badly. One of my best friends, and a man whom I greatly respect is the Reverend John MacKelvie, presently of Northwood, Middlesex, and he has so often underlined the dignity with which church members known to him have died that I often wonder if we live in the same world. 'My own' Presbyterians usually laboured under a chilly puritanism which seemed unable to visualise anything convincing to see them through the final chapter. Even my father, during his later years, began to feel that 'the church offered nothing', and that in spite of his lifetime of attendance. He died a reluctant agnostic, or, at best, a very doubting Christian with many reservations.

By contrast, it became increasingly easy to find common ground with local Catholic priests, even if I disagreed with their attitudes towards children of mixed marriages or to contraception. At least their views were the views of their Church, but I often wondered if the Church of Scotland had passionate views about anything except to keep out bishops or pay only official lip service to the ecumenical movement. So far as giving emotional assistance at the bedside of a dying man was concerned it was, and within my experience, generally fairly useless. Most of my parson friends had as many doubts as their flock and they all had my sympathy. I found it especially sad that *their minds seemed closed to all historical records which did not fit in with their training* while the licence which they used to interpret biblical texts or stories was breath-taking in its audacity.

It seemed obvious that human beings did have a soul, a spirit, or call it what one will. Nothing is so dead as a dead person, yet only a fraction of a second earlier, that same person had had personality, often a glint of humour or courage or hope, somehow a *presence* and, even if desperately demoralised after a long terminal illness, was still a human being with whom one could identify. During the split second of death it seemed to me that the body suddenly became a house without an occupant, flesh without spirit, an object. *Something had gone out of him.*

Two personal experiences, involving communication with Trudie from another country and during unexpected moments of danger to either her or one of our boys, had reinforced my belief that supra-normal experiences did exist, but that they existed only on a spiritual level: at a level involving the soul (for want of any other word). There had been no question of telepathy, spiritualism, or any other 'ism'. Our experiences were provable in a court of law and had been important, so I did, and do, believe in the soul.

I also believed, and still believe, in my childhood fairy who had proven that there could be active life on another dimension.

I cannot pin-point the month, or even the year, when I consciously rejected the divinity of Christ or certain basics of the Christian faith, but I do know that when I did I was freed from a burden of concern to 'justify' and 'explain' teachings and events which do not stand up to the criteria of historical or anthropological analysis. They don't, in fact, stand up to any analysis.

Increasing awareness of more primitive attitudes to death in Amazonia, Asia, or parts of Africa had made me suspect most of the teaching and the entire machinery of the Church. I believed that truth had been 'angled' at various precise points in time, and for quite specific reasons, and I began to accept, without reservation, the validity of old matriarchal religions which had, in a sense, survived within the Catholic Church and various other places after beginnings deep in pre-history. I saw, in Mary, the old Goddess, who had played one part as Mother. Mary Magdalene (the young adoptive mother) had also been at the Cross and I saw in that Mary the same Goddess as Mistress. While in Salome* I saw the traditional 'layer-out', the death figure, the Goddess of the waning year who had also been the first person to adore the child Jesus, just as I also saw Jesus as a historical harvest Tammuz or Dionysus figure around whom all had to act out a traditional role. Nor could I forget that Jesus had been crowned King of Israel using the old formula preserved in the 'Coronation' psalm, and that this made him titular *son* of Apollo the *Sun-God*.

I had also come to realise from time to time, that I had grown close to the Goddess, and on a day when I met a teen-age girl, a friend of my son Craig, I even 'felt' her 'power' from that most unexpected source. Indeed, I wrote a poem within minutes of meeting her. She was dressed in purple, her name was Tessa, and she preferred to be known as Tristessa. She had deep knowledge of many subjects, and such an awareness of so many important philosophical problems as could only be explained in a sixteen-year-old by close-to-the surface memory.

I had no doubts about life after physical death, and was able to comfort many people. I was also certain that further expansion of life would be constructive and active, that I would not be separated from Trudie, from our dogs, or from various people who showed empathy and 'knew us'. I even understood how this next phase would have different emotional values, that periods of training would be required, and that the experience would be rather wonderful. This conviction somehow came across to various dying bodies and I felt better for having made some hours glad with certainty. Not that I ever said much, and there was no spoken prayer since spoken prayer is censored and as such must be 'angled' or insincere. I am more concerned with *unspoken thoughts* and *unwhispered desires*. When these are

* *Mark*, Chapter XV.

189

translated into words censorship starts right at the subconscious threshold and the end product is a mere formal address. I did accept that Jesus had probably been divinely inspired, though he was not the 'son' of God. After all, the word 'son' is still used all over the Middle East and does not need to imply any bond relationship deeper than that of friend. Nor was the 'god' who inspired him much related to the Judaeo-Christian concept of 'God'.

I remembered Evangeline Booth who had 'saved me' in Mauchline. She was sincere, and there *are* many ways to the house with many mansions, but now I really *did* and do feel 'saved' – an unsuitable cliché. I also knew that Trudie had largely been responsible, and that we were pledged together for as much of eternity as we might deserve. I even sensed (with no wishful-thinking element) that it would be a long, long time, and that it had come about chiefly through involvement with a wife whose wisdom had blended with other wisdom gained from relatively undeveloped far-away places.

'New' doctors had succeeded my brother, but few had lasted long and had quit because of low income although they reached 'equal shares' in two years or less. Andrew Taylor and I had been the only practitioners in the town to accept offer of facilities within a Health Centre due to be built if we agreed to work within it, and even that prospect now seemed unimportant. Eventual fusion of our practice with that of two other men was equally irrelevant within the scheme of my own inward life since I was much more concerned with other matters.

A ten week Asiatic journey had taken Trudie and me from tea and good conversation with the Shah of Persia through Pakistan to Kashmir, and after meetings with (then) President Ayub Khan and Mr Buttho, to Hunza in a remote Karakorum-Himalayan valley. Hunza was the prototype of Shangri-la and we absorbed enough to understand why. A long tour through what is now Bangla Desh also made me despair more than ever of being able to give privileged people any standard of comparison. Grangemouth, measured against East Pakistan, was the land of Goshen ten times over. Yet did people in Britain appreciate their privileges? Our trip had rounded off with time to think in Jordan and Jerusalem, Nazareth and Bethlehem, where little impressed us. We could visualise it as the birth area of Armageddon without difficulty, but it was impossible to accept Bethlehem-Jerusalem as launching pads for a Prince of Peace. I felt no sympathy or attraction for a Church divided, and again admitted to myself that I was anti-ecclesiastic. It went without saying that I was also anti-Organisation, nor had I much in common with Abou Ben Adhem who loved *all* his fellow men. All had my compassion, but it was impossible to love those of my tribe whose latest household values and private gods were increasingly different from everything we respected. Which made our treasured few friends increasingly important.

My mother suddenly died when we were in Pakistan and near the disputed zone with India. I was sorry that she did not live to see Trudie having tea with Mohammed Ali Shah Pahlevi. Or with President Ayub. Or with H.E. of Kashmir and others. She would have been pleased!

Patients were now unobtrusively kind, but there were new-style practice problems. Personality clashes clanged like armour on a jousting field of old and only loyalty to my father prevented me from withdrawing. The new appointment system was a clear and final death-knell to efficiency. I had opposed it to the limit, but when forced to accept I knew that the end was near. The local Dyer-Alexander firm had rejected the original Health Centre concept but they to seemed to have developed problems and it suited us all well enough to fuse and operate from the Centre being built because of my own firm's co-operation. But I could hardly have cared less. I had little in common with our two new partners, and we did not even share similar views on various fundamental principles. James Dyer is small, plump, semi-jovial and built into the Grangemouth scene after a lifetime which began as assistant to that Doctor Anderson whose practice we had taken over. It was vaguely, and pseudo-sentimentally agreeable to see the two practices come together, since I like completing circles. It was also a pleasantly definitive sort of thing to contrive at that stage in time. Kenneth Alexander is a small man. Between us we must have had around 14,000 patients, and it was about 8,000 too many from my point of view.

We also used four secretaries, and my favourite was Sadie

Penman, then a candid seventeen-year-old who eventually and wisely withdrew and finally married a G.I. from Viet Namh after an invigorating year or so as an *au pair* in Paris. She was a local girl, but she too had no more in common with her tribe than an Eskimo would have had with Genghis Khan. I like to remember that she is now 'living happily ever after', and to know that she is still a friend.

But 1963 to 1968 were really productive years on other fronts. There was an annual David Grant spy thriller; the lecture circuit remained challenging; television activity increased and the John Toye *Today is* programmes were fun, while Bill Tennent's occasional interview was a valued contact with a likeable man: P and O continued to use us at least twice in the year, and I became a member of everything from the Mystery Writers of America and the Crime Writers Association through Int. P.E.N., the Society of Authors and the Guild of Travel Writers. I even found myself listed in *Who's Who in Europe* and eventually in Volume 10 of the *Dictionary of International Biography*.

An odd situation finally decided everything. Bouts of sickness and pain developed when involved with certain patients and I also developed a crippling limp. After months of regular attendance at the orthopaedic clinic pundits diagnosed a prolapsed intra-vertebral disc, provided me with a corset and allowed me to try and get on with the job. Sadly, however, old-style nightmares had returned to plague me as well.

The whole symptom complex had developed weeks after a two month research in South East Asia involving some hard sessions in both Cambodia and Viet Namh but I did not believe that the trip had anything to do with it. Nor had a period in Nepal where I had investigated the 'drop-out', 'beatnik', and 'drug' scene. The fact was, that dreams or sickness apart, the hip and leg pains made active life impossible. I was, by late November, 1968 almost completely incapacitated.

My father had also died a short while earlier when I was pointing for the West Indies during a P and O cruise, so I had missed the ends of both my parents and was glad only that I had seen doctoring through for so long. I had finally come to the end of my tether, but at least I had not caused them too much disappointment. The 'signpost' for which I had waited so long had come at last.

I ended a busy surgery one gusty November evening in 1968. Arrangements had been made to lie up with Trudie at Sesimbra, near Lisbon, and to try to recuperate for a couple of weeks. We were due to leave two days later and Alistair was booked to serve as locum. Dr Kenneth Alexander, however, disagreed not only with my choice of doctor to look after my health problem but said on the phone that he would not agree to my taking sick-leave and ordered me back to work. This was all rather silly, since he is very much my junior, had not the very slightest authority over me and must have known that I was operating strictly within the terms of our practice agreement.

The situation was farcical, clearly I had free choice of doctor, and my doctors were highly respected. It was also quite impossible for me to work. I could not even get into a car, far less climb stairs. At 54 I seemed to be a wreck, and I was even attending a hospital out-patient orthopaedic clinic.

I really could not be bothered talking with the man and hung up.

I did not return, and flew next day from Glasgow to Lisbon.

I notified the Medical Practices Committee, officially, that I was resigning and would be off work indefinitely. There was no alternative since I had also consulted my old colleague Archie MacPhater, a senior consultant physician in Glasgow Victoria, who diagnosed reactive depression. Other people then confirmed that Professor MacAlman's early assessment in the forties had been accurate. Medicine had continuously repelled me, and I had over-compensated for too long. The new life which I had been building up as an escape hatch to freedom was, experts said, more suitable. The fact that my leg began to mend almost as soon as I quit medicine confirmed their diagnosis. It disappeared almost on the day after my resignation finally expired. Which may have been coincidence, but it seemed a faultless example of a psychosomatic problem cured by removing the underlying cause. Psychiatrists assured me that there was nothing psychotic about my condition and that the only miracle lay in how I had endured a medical career for so long.

Less than two years later Alistair had two supposedly minor

coronary episodes, and it began to seem as though two sons were paying a high price for the ambitions of their parents. Trudie and I were happy that we had taken steps to act very differently with our own two boys, and were content with the outcome to date.

Our eldest had gone to Turkey for one whole year when only eighteen and lived close to the ground in a village still remote from development, but surrounded by sites of unexploited antiquarian interest. He had returned fit and well, with a new competence and self-reliance. Above all, he had valid standards of comparison and was less likely to take his own privileges in life for granted. Turkey, we believed (and still do) had given him stature. He had learned more about morality and the importance of honour, service, hard work, and the emotional importance of quality labour in a remote wind-swept Anatolian village than he had done after seventeen years in highly-privileged Britain where so much was now taken as an entitlement.

Leonard, too, had made the same trip solo and spent around three months in the same area, but he had travelled to other interesting places using his own initiative and collecting his own standards. Pre-tourist Sardinia, Holland, Yugoslavia, Anatolia and Istanbul had all left their mark. New friendships and knowledge had also opened up new horizons. He had, and has, a reassuring quiet strength.

We knew that our two young men would not go far wrong, but the fact remained that their 'norms' had been acquired among tribes very different from their own.

As for ourselves! There was a new sense of freedom. We had been obliged to struggle for a long time before being quit of any need to consider the desires of parents who wanted too much. We were glad that we had allowed our own two sons to frame their lives and choose their own friends without anxiety about our reactions. In the event, they both opted to do a sensible thing and acquired B.A.s at Stirling University before finally making up their minds as to which of life's many doors they would open to make a living. Which is, as it should be. We provided varied opportunities to learn, but we exerted no compulsion to use them.

We were also pleased to understand how, right from the

194

beginning, our boys saw through the nonsense of anti-permissive society campaigns. As Craig so wisely said, 'when I read the Sunday papers it seems to me that it is adults who are immoral, not youth. The Organisation is only trying to divert public attention away from things which really *are* permissive, and which really do matter.'

I knew exactly what he meant. If family doctoring had taught me anything it was the extent to which people were hypocrites. But it had also revealed how easily a majority could be swayed by angled propaganda operating on their lack of imagination, their prejudices, fears and greed. Little wonder, I thought, that neither priests nor doctors could be taught at university level about the *real* human situation.

One afternoon, in Sesimbra, I saw another series of memory pictures, the first since leaving Kilmarnock, but these were minor dramas mostly covering the family doctor scene.

Families driven to sedatives by vindictive neighbours!

Disputes about cleaning common stairways, keeping common gardens tidy, or feuds about pets.

Men who had died and left no wills! I saw again flashes of families fighting over the few valuables remaining beside a dead parent, and in one case two sons beating each other in blind rage as each tried to seize a television set.

I also saw again people who had been in debt, and their fear of warrant sales; how Alistair or I had helped, in one case with upwards of eighty pounds, and how it had never been repaid, and how, within a few months the patient's daughter was having sessions at a nearby riding school equipped with full riding gear. Where, we had asked ourselves again and again, were there any principles left?

Rising class hatreds also flickered back into mind, though old-fashioned class-war mumbo-jumbo had long made me emotionally weary. 'Workers' wanted ever larger cuts from the national cake, and I knew from conversations uncountable, that they did not care how they got it or who suffered. The new god was self, and there was no other god. The new hell was to be slightly under-privileged by advanced British or European standards, and there was no other hell. The one still remaining commandment from other years was 'don't be found out'. Petty pilfering was so standard that it was taken for granted, and every local 'security man' in industry accepted that many already-big-money-'workers' organised thefts galore. While we all knew that ability to talk doctors into issuing certificates for non-existent illness which were difficult to disprove was a major status symbol.

I also glimpsed a fast run of stills showing lonely people unwanted by families who wished them dead.

While another series reminded me of the difficulty younger people had in organising relief from nursing an aged relative, and I watched the 'young folk' become prematurely aged as I had seen them so often in real life. On the other side of the coin I could not forget Britain's more general attitude to old people and knew that it would rate as a crime against humanity among many so-called primitive people, who not only grant senior citizens the status of wise elders, but see to it that they are never allowed to be lonely. Multi-million geriatric hospitals are really the modern state's answer to demands from people off-loading responsibility while seeking more and more 'fun', or else developing tension problems because they do not know what to do with their leisure.

An even longer series brought familiar faces back into focus as puzzled teenagers or children flickered into mind, and I knew that their wary eyes were asking the same questions. Why do the family not give me their time? Why do they nag me? Why don't they answer questions seriously when I'm needing advice?

Then there were a few young mothers fretting over their babies, or sitting in lonely rooms while their men screwed around in developing countries while not boring for oil, erecting bridges or cutting roads, and I marvelled at another extraordinary convention which seemed to have come down from the past. I had learned from their own lips how many men still thought that males had a licence to promiscuity while still demanding total loyalty from their wives.

Medicine had also taught me that women were still underprivileged on too many fronts. It was a tragi-comedy that the female caste with greatest deprivation was women married to men who were themselves hell-bent on bullying the state into making them very privileged, and who were members of the new £80 a week aristocracy.

Society was sick because of strange factors playing upon human frailty and perhaps it was harsh to blame 'ordinary' people – the great silent majority – for yielding to temptations which might well destroy our nation. There had been no inspired leadership from the top during my lifetime, excepting, of course, during the war, but Beveridge and those others who launched the welfare state had lacked experience of life and the vision to appreciate that they had only devised a malingerer's charter.

Self-discipline – and every form of discipline – had been ignored in all propaganda. No politician had ever been heard to deal with abstract essentials like love, compassion or the need for dedicated service – yet without these motivations how could there be anything but chaos?

Leaders of all parties indoctrinated the nation with the belief that possessions and money equated with happiness. But not even the left ever suggested that it had become grossly immoral for men who earned big money to demand more – and more – and more, while three fourths of the rest of the world struggled on, below, or just above the poverty line. When Ethiopia, with vast tracts of the African desert countries, the Indian subcontinent and millions within South America were confronted with near, or actual, famine not one leader within Britain ever suggested that any 1973 or 1974 salary increase be given, instead, as an act of compassion to those hundreds of millions who needed it more than they.

Work had become a four letter, dirty word.

Thoughts of service were anathema to many.

Class hatreds and colour prejudices, religious feuds and those even more deeply seated tensions born from 'territorial rights', and which made certain people feel maximally insecure when obliged to change address or job had split Britain apart at the seams and the country's leaders seemed to play everything by ear – hoping for a miracle.

As a professional traveller and observer I knew that friends abroad despaired for us, that enemies rejoiced, and that all marvelled how a nation could lose its soul, its pride and much of its reputation within twenty years. Yet the reason was simple. All those factors which played upon the post-war world had played upon continental European countries as well as upon Britain. We had not been given especial treatment by Fate, nor had unique forces from the outside world combined to humiliate us and us alone. Most observers knew, and knew well, that two situations had been chiefly instrumental in bringing about disaster – a succession of inadequate governments from both main parties; and a significant number of traitors holding positions of authority or trust in high places. The Philby story cast light upon one. And there are others. It is considered bad taste to refer to any politician who may have been a card carrying member of the Communist party in his younger days. Yet was not it standard teaching 'to profess false doctrines in order to gain positions of power' and to bring down by burrowing from within. Surely there had, in the interests of the majority, to be a curb upon so-called freedom and upon the legal right of a few men to destroy a country's economy, debase its reputation abroad and terrorise society.

'Ordinary' people had somehow been conditioned to believe that anyone speaking on television was almost divinely inspired; that political pronouncements at all levels must, if broadcast, be accurate; and only slowly had they begun to sense that their leaders were not only fallible but almost certainly inadequate to deal with the social quicksands which had been brought into being by equally inadequate predecessors thinking in terms of votes, class, political dogma and materialism.

Meanwhile, they would all buy time: first by using the Common Market tensions as an excuse. Metrication would be an added excuse when the time came to explain why things were going wrong. Since other European countries also had problems – even if not so sinister – it might suit everyone to evolve a common European currency, and that too would be excuse enough to buy still more time and give more reasons as to why stability was still round the corner. Federation would follow some time later and the United States of Europe would, assuredly, have so many birth pangs that every political would find it easy to explain away almost anything. Meanwhile, Enoch Powell would be proven accurate enough in some of his judgements, and parts of Europe, including Britain, would slowly become honey – or coffee-coloured. Cheap foreign labour used in

Germany and elsewhere would not remain celibate and Middle Europe would blend, to some extent, with the Middle East and Iberia. Holland, which had admitted so many people from her Indies – both East and West – would also become permanently sunburned.

One tragedy, however, would linger, as I had already proved in other places – the colour question would not, even then, be resolved: those with the lighter coloured skins would regard darker skins as belonging to second class citizens. And in some respects this saddened me more than anything else, because given a real blending of the nations something good might well emerge. But the question remained – what is 'good'?

The answer to this seemed to become the crux of the whole matter. 'Good' was an elusive target. Possibly 'goodness' was even a dangerous ideal because, within my own lifetime, I had lived with the disastrous results of do-gooders divorced from reality. Between them all they had made crime pay, created a nation of disease-conscious neurotics, promoted greed and generated class warfare on a scale verging upon revolution. On reflection I felt that Faith might be a better idea to strive for than Goodness. But of course politicals did not discuss Faith either! Faith, Soul, Love and Humility were non events in an election where appeals to greed, envy, self-interest and materialism were more likely to achieve results.

Unconscious instinct suddenly made me squirm when I realised how memory had concentrated only upon human faults or weaknesses and I wondered what sickness still made me so critical. Yet on the same mind-wandering level of back-thinking I realised that my thoughts were not far out of true perspective. I accepted that men and women were capable of magnificent self-sacrifice during peak moments of danger. I knew that many reacted with total disregard for consequences when faced with a life-saving emergency. I did not forget how some faced a life-time of sacrifice for a partner or for a principle and that a few were compulsive 'givers' whose generosity never seemed to fail. Yet I could not forget half a century of experience or a dream in which a god-symbol had reminded me how 'the world was mad, not bad' or how a 'few found Truth and walked alone' and how

> 'the world is ruled by fops and fools
> bluffing or playing by ear,
> while they help each other to break the rules
> as mediocrities cheer.'

Memory also continued to remind me that the god-symbol found men

[*as*]

> 'cheating to live! Afraid to die!
> Phoney, pathetic small men
> keep passing the buck, scared to say "why?"
> Or "Hi! Will you please explain."'

The fact remained that too many – probably a great majority – really did live with fear and simply opted out of contact with anything which threatened their own security. Worse, so-called civilisation accepted questionable things as worthy even if their use was against the best interests of the human species. There was, it seemed, a conflict between that which was good for the individual and that which was good for the whole. The word 'civilise' meant 'to refine' or 'to enlighten', yet modern 'civilisation' had created spiritual darkness by distorting values and confusing every moral issue. How, I asked, did it 'enlighten?' And it had created an infinite spectrum of physical pollution, while moral pollution which really mattered had little to do with sex but centred rather upon those sophisticated corruptions which tolerated political double talk, genocide, famine situations threat of global annihilation and dissemination of rumours calculated to generate fear or soft-treatment of evil criminals and the agnosticism which became inevitable when materialism placed a higher value upon worldly things than it did upon spiritual. Poverty favoured religion in one form or another. Prosperity favoured self-interest and rejection of the soul.

I fell asleep while the film strip flickered on in blazing technicolour and then I seemed to dream, but the dream became even more strange as I began to understand arguments which I knew would be rejected by almost everyone.

Practically everything which people thought was good was actually bad.

Demand for life, even development of special care units or sophisticated advances in every field of therapy was actually operating against chances of man's survival *as a species*. The 'thing' which might be good for an individual, might actually operate against survival of the whole. Death should be made easier, and not postponed as the world became increasingly over-crowded, otherwise the species would surely die. That apart, 'medicated survival', the living vegetable, was itself proof of man and medicine's distorted new values.

Medical ideas which were still in early experimental stages might even end by killing faith in the very conception of god or goddess. Primitive considerations of genetic surgery, and the possibility of creating superman by modifying genes using laser rays or other techniques before fertilisation within a test tube and under laboratory conditions, *might*, one day, create a man-made monster of incredible intellectual quality but with no soul.

Development of memory transplant experiments might eventually enable the memory of a genius to be synthesised and perpetuated within a small number of selected people required for special purposes by the State. The thought plunged my dreams into nightmare confusion, and I saw a race of men with no souls operating like computers, but with neither compassion or humanity, intellectual monsters juggling with the jig-saw puzzles of state requirements covering numbers of 'units' allowed to survive.

My visions slowly blended with light, as more gentle dreams seized by half-conscious imagination.

The new race of welfare state petty tyrants and industrial bullies, professional small men and frightened politicians was the last convulsive throwing out from an ice-cold self-deceiving puritanism devoid of love, promising only little hope, and offering comfort only to few. But I also saw another generation rising, and I realised that it might produce new hopes and new saviours: quiet young men and women whose slogan was 'make love, not war'. Man would be 'saved' if he was to be 'saved', by new people, by new kinds of people, but never by people grouped into fanatical institutions. Man just might be saved by self discipline, tolerance and love.

Love, however, did not mean only those youngsters, caressing one another with that awareness and sensitivity which was unknown to earlier generations, where all too many men virtually raped their brides on the marriage night: even in Grangemouth during the 60s! Ignorance of women's need was being replaced by thoughtful knowledge among the young. There was a new equality of the sexes and many were looking for a love which rose far above physical contacts. Most were lusting after compassion and peace.

A wind of candour which was blowing through the world of youth made me relax with deep content.

Perhaps I had sometimes tended to forget those many quiet people who still clung to important values, and perhaps I had thought too much about that anarchistic, nihilistic, acquisitive and lustful minority which spewed out so much trouble. But the silent majority was not, now, quite so silent. 'Awareness' was dawning and there were early signs of change even if too many were still afraid.

The booming travel world had, in spite of contriving obstacles to insulate visitors against locals, begun to contribute towards understanding. This, too, was a trend which would expand until it would become standard for Aberdeen fishermen or Midland carworkers to holiday on the beaches of Queensland or among Pacific Islands, just as they had in Majorca.

The rising new generation had also told me, again and again in my office, that the *real* permissive society was that mass of older people which had 'permitted' politically involved persons to manipulate argument and law to suit themselves; or that it was the society which was so deeply steeped in prejudice that employees with employers alike 'permitted' themselves to drift into situations which had debased our reputation and damaged our economy; or that it was the society which had ruined much of what was left of once lovely landscapes and sited ugly industry on the few remaining beauty spots of an already over-industrialised country. Youth had been blamed by guilty leaders for practically every crime from genocide in Viet Namh to endemic venereal disease, but the whole indictment was biased. Medicine had made me respect the young.

My father, perhaps, had been more wise than I realised. People *did* only know what they read, heard, saw or experienced, and he had known that without experience it was difficult for them to accept much. The rising new world was experiencing more by 25 than most parents had by 60, and they were acquiring not only some wisdom but also a longing for attachment to a Cause bigger than themselves. It was reassuring and I wakened up with Trudie smiling by my side.

'You look better,' she said.

'I feel better and I've learned a lot, but we've all paid a high price,' I added. 'Especially you. Think how much more happy you might have been if my life had taken a different course.'

She smiled. 'But then we wouldn't have been us, and it is us who matter. I only want one more thing in this life, because we've got everything else.' She paused. 'I've wanted to be a grandmother since before we were even married. Life *will* go on, and our children are solid. Lots of the new people are solid and the new Establishments should be different from those we used to know.' She pointed towards the open sea and at fishing boats bobbing in the distance which reminded me of *Fado* and my first cruise: *Fado*, that plaintive lamenting prayer in song by women asking for the impossible.

Somehow it seemed appropriate. Another circle had been completed. I had first visited Lisbon as a student when I began to study clinical medicine. What odd subconscious memory was it, I wondered, which had brought me back at that particular time when I had newly quit.

Trudie took my arm as we pointed up-hill to our rooms. 'You think too much. Just remember that we are "us" because of everything and everybody which has happened, but now we can live, and perhaps we shall become a different sort of "us".'

I wakened in the small hours that morning with an urgent need to write a poem.

> Circle round!
> Circle complete?
> Wisdom found?
> Yes. Wisdom replete
> with sorrow.

Passing years
and passing time,
fearful tears
all fearful, chime
tomorrow.

Years ahead
and years behind
memory, said
'Memories find
the soul.'

Hopeful hearts
all hopeful, plan
future charts.
A fate they CAN
control.

The Mother known!
Your Goddess wise
says 'humbly go
and humbly rise
to live.'

Heaven is free.
Heaven's at hand.
Only agree
Her one command.
'Forgive'.

It is a strange poem, but then it came at the end of a strange
and long-drawn-out chapter. Somewhere, deep within it, there
must be at least a shadow of the creatures whom Trudie called
'us'.

EPILOGUE

Confessions are painful and exposure of privacy can be even more so. Yet to make my confessions understandable and give point to what some say has been an eccentric career it became necessary to reveal at least a little of self.

After six years divorce from medicine it has been shattering to find how exposure to any medical situation provokes recurrence of hip pain, and sometimes within seconds. Request to see a sick child during an emergency in Fiji once made me limp back to my hut with a limp like an old man. A sudden need to give first-aid at a road-side accident triggered off immediate pain which lasted for several hours; and seven or eight similar experiences have further proved how deeply engrained that psychosomatic problem has become.

Yet, when I day-dream, my memory pictures are now vastly different and I awaken refreshed. Some flashes have recurred again and again until I actually look forward to reliving experiences which were good for both mind and body.

Our gardens glowing with colour while birds nest among flowering spring trees and young birds flirt in the sunshine.

Our squirrels waiting to be fed by a kitchen window.

Scarlet ibis flocking back from Venezuela to roost every evening by a lake in Trinidad, their flaming bodies daubing the blue sky with unforgettable colour.

A quiet beach in Tahiti bedecked with quietly singing girls stringing garlands of frangipani.

Laughing honey-coloured people from the Trobriand Islands where a still matriarchal society creates a special magic.

The vastness of Australia's desert and blood-red rocks around great gorges.

These, with ever-present visions of hill tribes in New Guinea smiling beneath head-dresses of feathers from Birds of Paradise, or the incredible beauty of life upon the Great Barrier Reef, the gentle music of children laughing on the Solomons and the purely white perfection of Nanga Parbat, the friendship of our sons with their wives and my knowledge that Trudie is happy all combine to make our new life a rare pleasure.

But we also live surrounded by tangible memories and treasure a small circle of friends whom we see all too seldom as we commute around the travel and lecture worlds. Even as I write I look upon framed panels of mandarin robes from old China and an aged ivory of a woman from Macau . . . a praying girl and a temple dancer worked in reddish black ebony from Bali sit together with a simply carved wooden pig from Melanesia . . . tiny statues from Italy blend with a few old plates upon a Flemish cabinet made when Rembrandt was young . . . a panel of French tapestry looks down upon prayer rugs from Turkey, while a vase behind my head, a poor pottery thing brought from Lisbon in 1933, stands beside a portrait of my wife. Photographs of the family's peak moments hang around my study together with a bronze cross from Byzantium and a head of Christ carved for me by an Austrian artist long ago, while a black cut-out of a limbo-dancer has been nailed above my study door and returns me daily to the West Indies and to the laughing dark people whom I love.

The whole situation has developed without plan or intention. We bring home a small thing which 'matters' and somehow we find a place for it.

This, somehow, has become symbolic.

Maybe there is a place for everything. Even for human folly.

Perhaps wisdom is to accept an over-all situation and be resigned.

Perhaps an even greater wisdom is to allow one's children to shape their own lives and make their own mistakes. Or even to allow them simply to 'waste time'. Given a little faith and a little luck it is just possible that 'time-waste' may be the most worthwhile thing they ever do.

Given, of course, knowledge that they are loved. Do not we all do so much better when we know that we are loved? And forgiven.

My brother Alistair has been mentioned throughout these confessions and I end with one of his poems.

I had a dream.
Stupid to dream
after a life
of watching dreams of other men
be killed,
or scorned
or trodden on
by feet of other men who could not dream.

Yet –
I had a dream.
That in itself
means hope.
If I can dream,
then so can others.
And so, some day,
this stricken world
may be so full of dreamers
that the few remaining men
who cannot dream
will be so filled with wonder
that they shall not
kill their brothers.

INDEX

211

213

214